We Ate Wonder Bread

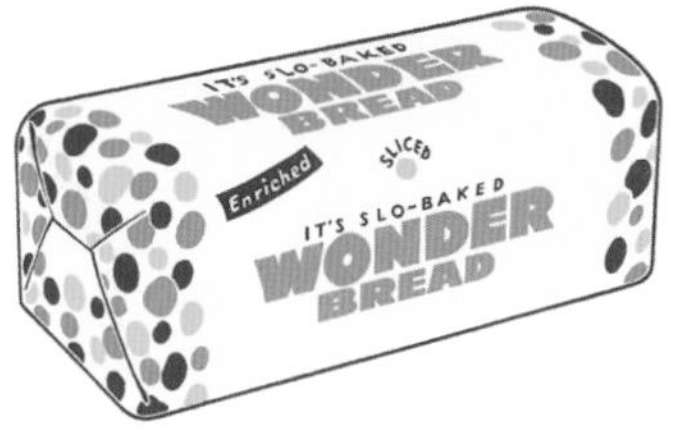
IT'S SLO-BAKED
WONDER
BREAD
SLICED
Enriched
IT'S SLO-BAKED
WONDER
BREAD

BOOKS BY NICOLE HOLLANDER

I'm in Training to Be Tall and Blonde

Ma, Can I Be a Feminist and Still Like Men?

That Woman Must Be on Drugs

*My Weight Is Always Perfect for My Height—
Which Varies*

*Mercy, It's the Revolution and I'm in
My Bathrobe*

Sylvia on Sundays

Hi, This is Sylvia

Okay, Thinner Thighs for Everyone

Never Tell Your Mother This Dream

The Whole Enchilada

Never Take Your Cat to a Salad Bar

You Can't Take it With You, So Eat It Now

Tales From the Planet Sylvia

Everything Here Is Mine

Female Problems: An Unhelpful Guide

My Cat's Not Fat, He's Just Big-Boned

Cats With Attitude

*Tales of Graceful Aging From
the Planet Denial*

The Sylvia Chronicles

We Ate Wonder Bread

A MEMOIR OF GROWING UP ON THE WEST SIDE OF CHICAGO

BY NICOLE HOLLANDER

FANTAGRAPHICS BOOKS

Editor: Gary Groth
Production: Paul Baresh
Associate Publisher: Eric Reynolds
Publisher: Gary Groth

Fantagraphics Books, Inc.
7563 Lake City Way NE
Seattle, WA 98115
www.fantagraphics.com

ISBN: 978-1-68396-010-2
Library of Congress Control Number: 2016961056
First Printing: March 2018
Printed in China

To my father, who took me along when he joined the Carpenters Union and who started me thinking about who had power and who was dispossessed.

To Shirley and Esther and Olga, who were strong, witty women, and to all of us who were waiting for feminism for all of our lives and embraced it wholeheartedly when it arrived.

To Tom, my brilliant and long-suffering designer, and June, my brilliant and long-suffering editor.

To Lyn, my agent who brought me to Fantagraphics, and to Gary Groth, who perservered to make it a better book.

Introduction

BY ALISON BECHDEL

This book is indeed, as the subtitle states, a memoir of Nicole Hollander's childhood on Chicago's West Side. But as you begin reading, it will become clear to you by page seven that *We Ate Wonder Bread* is also a superhero origin story. The star of Hollander's long-running comic strip *Sylvia* is perhaps not technically a superhero, but she was a heroine to me and she certainly possesses powers far beyond those of mere mortals. (Among them, supreme confidence mixed with kindness, a steadfast loyalty to her friends, and the ability to look good in absolutely any kind of headgear—from a snood to a babushka to a Carmen Miranda fruit assemblage.)

"No one had babysitters," Nicole explains. "What I remember so vividly is being part of the life of my mother and her friends—Shirley, Esther, and Olga." There's a photo of a tiny Nicole laughing delightedly at something being said by a tough, pretty woman with the deadpan expression of a seasoned Borscht-Belt comic—Esther—witheringly exhaling a cloud of cigarette smoke.

From the raucous banter of these mesmerizing women, Sylvia clearly sprang fully-formed and ready for repartee. Here too is the origin of her progressive political bent—Nicole's father listening to right-wing talk radio because, "It's important to know what they're up to." In fact, here is the origin of Sylvia's sidekick Harry, the bartender who lives downstairs from her. But here Harry is the gangster who lives downstairs and pays Nicole to package the magic tricks he sells on the side.

As Nicole's vivid recollections proliferate, it's hard to imagine anyone growing up in this place not becoming a cartoonist. She has a close call involving a poodle skirt. Her sister gets a coat hanger stuck in her eye. Her mother smokes with the ashtray resting on her pregnant belly. The kitchen is stocked with Lady Aster brand schmaltz.

The stories flow thick and fast, and seem almost animated thanks to the many, many illustrations that spill across the pages. Hollander's vibrant crayon drawings augment and elucidate the text, but have their own delicious internal logic.

Sylvia paved the way for later generations of women cartoonists, but it was life in a chaotic, joke-filled West Side six-flat that paved the way for *Sylvia*. Get comfortable, because you're not going to be able to put this book down until you've finished it.

The Courtyard

WHERE IT ALL BEGAN

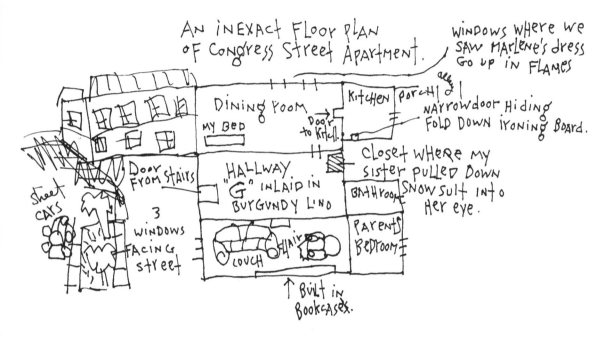

AN INEXACT FLOOR PLAN
OF CONGRESS Street Apartment.

WINDOWS WHERE WE
SAW MARLENE'S dress
GO UP IN FLAMES

DINING ROOM

MY BED

Door to Kitch.

KITCHEN PORCH

NArrowdoor Hiding
FOLD DOWN IRONING Board.

Door From Stairs

HALLWAY.
"G" INLAID IN
BURGUNDY LINO

Closet WHERE MY
Sister PULLED DOWN
SNOW suit INTO
Her eye.

BATHROOM

Street CARS

3
WINDOWS
FACING
street

COUCH CHAIR

PARENTS
BEDROOM

↑ Built in
Bookcases.

idly type my childhood address into the computer: 3914 W. Congress Street, Chicago. My block appears before me, whole and intact. Memories come flooding back.

I see the courtyard where we lived and the policeman coming up the walk to find my scofflaw father and Harry, the loan shark who lived on the first floor, and I see my sister pull down her snowsuit from the hall closet and see it land on her face, hanger and all, and her calmly walking to the kitchen to my mother with the snowsuit hanging from her lower eyelid. I see Marilyn on the top floor, her virtue protected by her parents and her lavish bedroom, and I hear her crying in our kitchen to my mother and father that her boyfriend has nude photographs of her.

I have been back to the old neigh-borhood, to my school, where as a child I

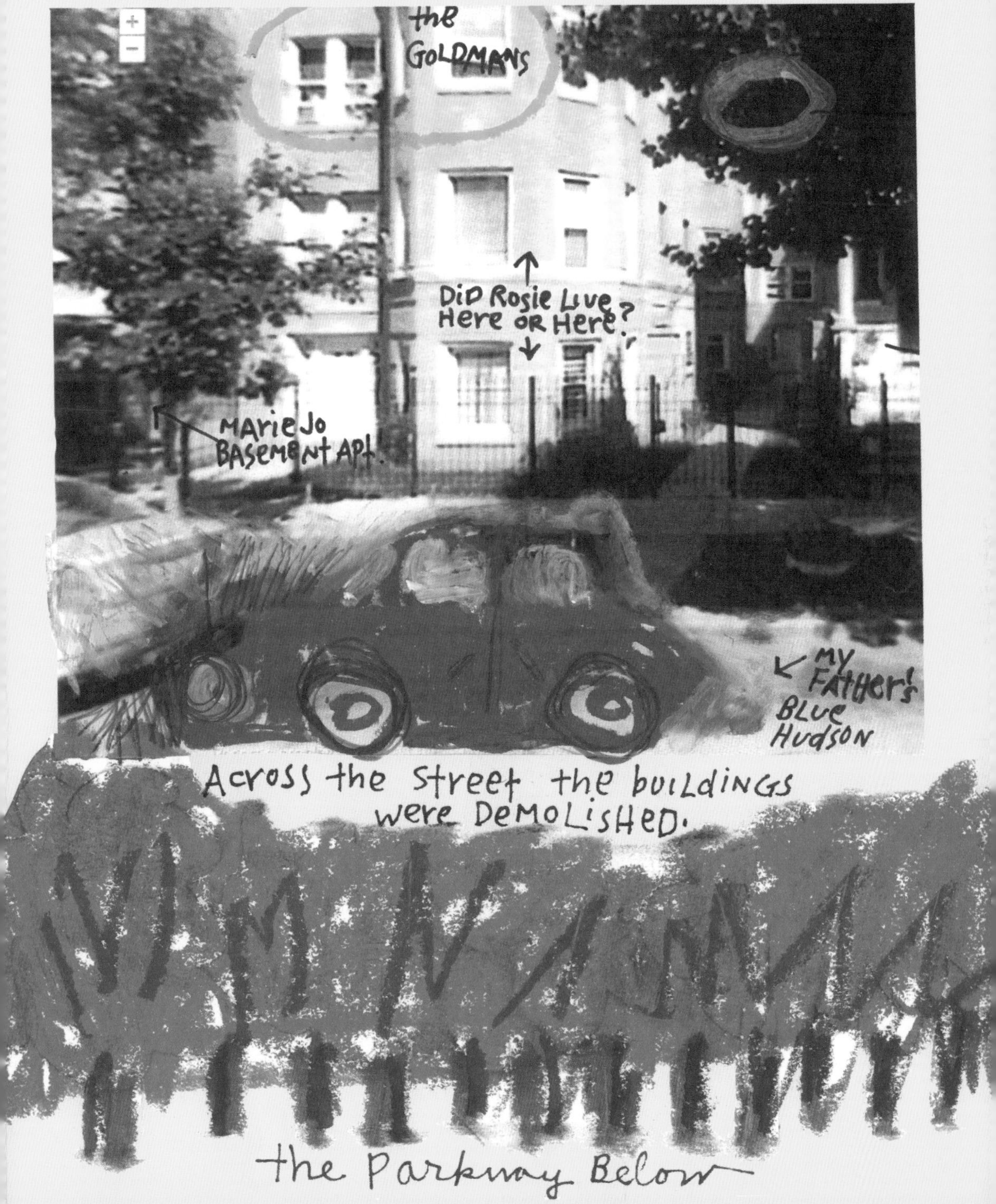
the GOLDMANS
DID Rosie Live Here or Here?
Marie Jo BASEMENT APT.
MY FATHER'S BLUE HUDSON
Across the street the buildings were DEMOLISHED.
the Parkway Below

had lunch at my aunt's house every day while my cousin tormented me with a scary voice behind his comic book.

On this block of Adams only two buildings remain, alone, two monoliths in a grassy field. The candy store on Pulaski Road is gone, the block is gone. The ma and pa grocery store on the corner of Pulaski and Congress where I was accused of killing Jesus is gone, replaced by a Citgo station.

Learning to Dis

HOW I FOUND SYLVIA

WE INVENT A CHARACTER CALLED GLADYS TO "DIS" TRYING TO SOUND LIKE OUR MOTHERS

GLADYS WEARS UGLY SHOES.

GLADYS IS A DOPE.

← OLGA'S DAUGHTER JACKIE HAS RED HAIR. I WONDERED WHY SOME JEWS HAD RED HAIR, NOW I THINK I KNOW.

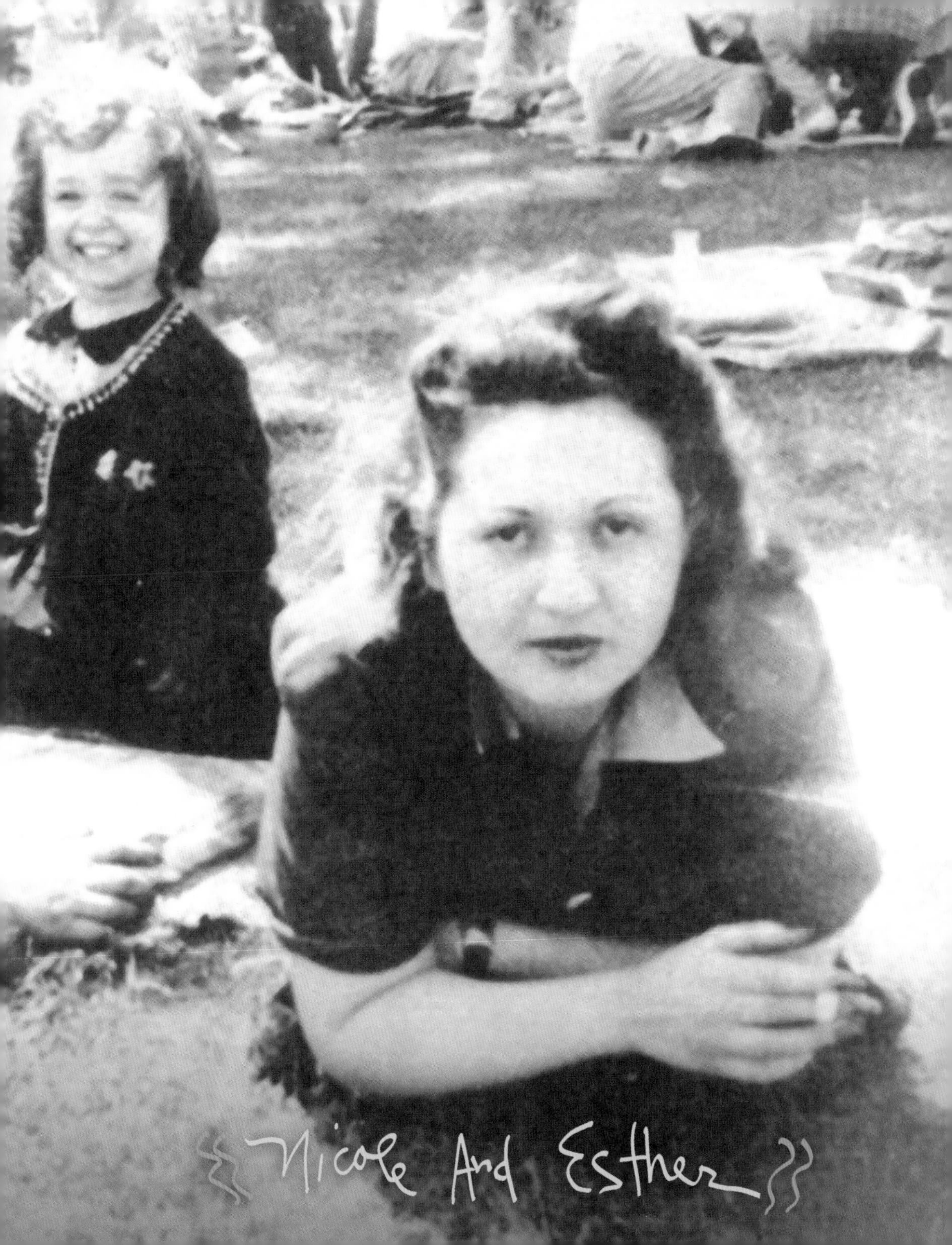
{{ Nicole And Esther }}

No one had babysitters. Neither of my grandmothers had any interest in taking care of their grandchildren in the evenings. I'm sure my maternal grandmother and grandfather had a poker game to attend. My paternal grandmother had quite a few grandchildren, and if she started babysitting where would it end?

Lack of babysitters didn't seem to be a problem. We just went everywhere with our mothers. The legend was that when we were babies, we were just parked in a dresser drawer when a party was going on and slept peacefully among the revelers.

What I remember so vividly is being part of the life of my mother and her friends—Shirley, Esther, and Olga. They took us to lunch with them. We were three girls about the same age. We were not part of their conversation but we were avid listeners, fearful of interfering with their talk, hoping they wouldn't notice us so they would keep on talking. They were all witty women, fiercely loyal to their friendship, to the specialness of every woman in the group. They had known each other as teenagers, selling magazine subscriptions door to door. They married men from the same social club and had daughters around the same time.

My mother would dis someone for not getting up in the morning to get her child off to school or to give her a good breakfast. Esther would look at her dryly and say, "I don't get up until noon. My daughter has instructions to let me sleep even if the building is on fire." My mother would say, "But that's you." The subtext was, "All of you are special and cannot sin in my eyes." My mother had a quick wit. Esther was the bad girl. She and her pal Edie would run off for weekends in New York, and come back, invigorated, talking about their sexual exploits. We kids were excluded from these conversations.

Olga and Esther were built alike: long legs, high waists, and buxom. Olga could tell jokes. She remembered punch lines. There was no way my mother could remember the beginning, middle, or end of a joke.

Olga came from a huge Russian family. There was always a party at her house and she remembered what everyone liked to eat. The family members were verbal Communists, all talk. They yelled their politics. Olga's husband Frank made a "good living"—he sold novelty items. He and Esther's husband

Lew hardly spoke a word from one year to the next.

My father seemed dashing compared to them. He flirted, he danced. He earned hardly any money. Now my memories of my father seem unstoppable: My father could sing. Before his voice changed he sang in the choir at the synagogue. Later he sang to us: "His actions were graceful, the girls he did please… the man on the flying trapeze" and "Sam, you made the

16

suit and vest fit the best, but Sam, you made the pants too long!"

When he and his buddies went to a friend's wedding they would sit in the back and yell at the groom, "Don't do it! You're making a mistake!" Meanwhile, my mother and I would sit as far away from them as possible. My mother was dissing the bride, her dress, her face, etc. I would start giggling. She said sternly, "Look at your nails!" That is her cure for

giggling inappropriately. This advice is only sometimes useful, much like her cure for hiccups: 1. Swallow a teaspoon of sugar. (This one works well, actually.) 2. Drink water from the opposite side of the glass. This is impossible but may distract you from hiccupping.

Olga told me once that my father called her and said, "I'm in love with you." She said, "No, you're not," and hung up on him. She adored her husband, but he wasn't very sexual, or at least not enough for her. Perhaps my father thought this meant he could step in, but he had misjudged the situation.

Olga also told me that my father never offered to pick anyone up. Telling her he loved her and not being accommodating were her two criticisms of him. I was surprised that he never offered to drive anyone anywhere, because I thought of him and his car as inseparable.

Once he dropped me off in the neighborhood at Clark and Devon. It was after we left Lawndale, when we lived in Rogers Park. I was wearing a big poodle skirt. I jumped out of the car, but not all of my skirt came with me. I was caught by the car door. He began to drive away and I ran alongside the car, banging on the window until he noticed me. He was shaken.

Sylvia was conceived in the old neighborhood. If my mother hadn't had her friend Esther and if women hadn't taken their daughters with them everywhere, I would never have heard their stories and made their language my own.

I KNEW YOU AS A CHILD.

YOU LOOK LIKE MY MOTHER'S FRIEND, ESTHER.

The Dining Room

WHERE EVERYTHING HAPPENED

SLEEPING IN THE DINING ROOM

When the dining room was my bedroom, the door between the kitchen and the dining room was closed. Everyone liked to hang out in the kitchen.

ASLEEP.

FULLY AWAKE

Is that the sound of sobbing coming from the kitchen? Is that Marilyn spilling her guts? Must Get Closer!

The dining room on Congress Street was the place where everything happened. At night it served as my bedroom, where I slept on a twin bed that came with bed bugs, which I hunted down. I attached them to little wooden carts with twine. Well, not really.

I played double solitaire with my grandmother at the dining room table. My maternal grandparents played poker with their friends at that same table. I hid under it with a blue-eyed child who should have been my brother, but he was sent back. I witnessed Marlene in flames out of the dining room windows and I saw my mother have a bloody miscarriage on what was my bed at night (which led to attempts like the blue-eyed boy to increase our family). I had my graduation party there and at night I listened at the kitchen door to Marilyn's sobbing about her perfidious boyfriend and the nude photos.

There was no molding, little decoration in the apartment, nothing on the walls except a framed print of a full-masted sailing ship rolling in rough waters on the living room wall. How sad. How did I ever learn about color? I must have discovered color at school, just as I discovered reading and didn't discover math. Or perhaps it was the influence of my friend's mother who lived a few blocks away. (Those blocks were crucial in income and status.) Ann's mother had a drawer full of filmy colored material, swishy and luxurious, that we dressed up in and pretended to be Isadora Duncan. Ann was allowed to eat dinner, SpaghettiO's, right out of the can. Unheated. Ann's mother was my first bohemian.

Our apartment was unadorned except for a small chandelier in the center of the dining room ceiling with

CHANDELIER
the INVADERS

this IS MY BED.

Here I AM IN the dining ROOM.

DINING ROOM table

MY ALMOST brother eating 1/4 lb of UNSALTED BUTTER.

* He HAS the bluest eyes.

LISTENING AT THE KITCHEN DOOR

I listened at the kitchen door until my fear of discovery drove me back to bed.

MARILYN SOBS: "He's BLACKMAILING ME! MY PAReNts will Die oF SHame"

MARiLYN SAYS: "MY PAReNts WiLL KiLL Me" AND MY FATHer SAYiNG "I'Ll Set him STraiGHt."

tear-shaped crystals. Once a month my mother prepared a mixture of vinegar and water and placed it in a bowl on the dining room table. I stood on the table and removed each crystal tear and dipped it in the mixture. The pendants were attached to the chandelier with hooks. I often cut myself while removing them or putting them back. It was worth it for the display of color when the sun hit the sparkling crystals.

The only other interesting feature of the apartment was a narrow door in the kitchen that hid a foldout ironing board. I have one now. They come ready-made in a wooden box and you just attach them to the wall. I was prepared to have a hole cut in the wall and have one fitted in. I had no idea that other secret ironing board lovers like me created a demand for them and they were available at Home Depot.

Serious things happened in the dining room. My mother has a miscarriage. She worries that the blood will ruin her robe. This happens on my bed. The neighbors come over and I am sent away. But I return, unable to leave her.

My parents try to foster two boys, on separate occasions. Finally my mother becomes pregnant with my sister. The crib is in the one bedroom. My mother dresses in the dark so as not to wake the baby. She goes to work with one navy blue shoe and one black.

And then one day he was gone

I have my grammar school graduation party in the dining room. The table is moved under the window and covered with a tablecloth, which is covered with food. I have a pink dress with a long skirt. My bed is pushed to the side and disguised.

My grandparents play poker in the dining room. They tease each other. The dealer keeps up a patter: "Possible straight, possible full house, possible nothing!" My paternal grandmother Annie plays ferocious double solitaire with me at that table.

My mother smoked during pregnancy. I believe every pregnant woman did. There was no thought of harming the fetus. Maybe they thought they still looked sexy even though very pregnant if they had a Pall Mall between their fingers. Perhaps they thought smoking had a calming effect on both the child and the mother.

My mother would balance an ashtray on her huge belly and ask me to observe how the baby bouncing in the womb would move the ashtray up and down.

In the age of no television for most families, this was endlessly amusing. Now it is possible that this would be an Internet meme, contests run to see which baby could move the ashtray higher. What am I saying? My mother would have been arrested, my sister would have been born in prison and I would have gone to an orphanage, where I would have learned math, become a CPA, and my colored pencils would have been smashed to smithereens and thrown away.

BAD DAD

A DIFFICULT MAN

I PUT "the Carpenter" on the PHONE.* voice dripping with IRONY, DISDAIN.."

*MY FATHER HAD A FAILED CONSTRUCTION BUSINESS

There is a uniformed policeman coming up the walk in the courtyard of our yellow brick building on Congress Street. I ask a neighbor what is happening. Quick as a whip she says, "He's selling tickets to the Policemen's Ball."

Why was I curious—did I have a feeling of impending disaster at the sight of a policeman? Did she lie automatically to protect me?

My father had a number of bad habits. One was to graciously accept a speeding ticket from a policeman through his rolled-down window and then tear it into many tiny pieces and throw it out the window in time for the policeman to see the pieces flutter into the air. It was a spectacle, satisfy-ing in that it confirmed that my father was afraid of nothing or at least gave no thought to the results of his actions. Yes, I enjoyed it.

I'M NOT SCARED OF YOU*

*I WAS.

I think it was this kind of behavior that made me think he was a god. He was a fearsome god also, with a bad temper. Once I told him to go to hell. "I'm not scared of you." I was. He smiled a scary smile and asked my aunt, "Did you hear that?" She said, "I'm sure she didn't mean it."

On weekends my father liked to drive. He drove out to the country. I don't know if he had any idea where he was going. The movement was the thing. To us, getting out of the house without a terrible scene was the thing. This was rare.

I remember what I am wearing on this weekend because it is the occasion for an outburst. I am wearing a navy blue suit and a white blouse with a large collar. The blouse has cuffs. I remember the outfit and my hairstyle because I have a studio portrait of it. It must have been my graduation outfit. My father notices that the collar and cuffs are not clean! He begins to shout that they have to be taken off and cleaned.

The amazing part of this story is that my mother makes no move to help.

HE SMILED A SCARY SMILE AND ASKED MY AUNT: "DID YOU HEAR THAT?"

I'M SURE SHE DIDN'T MEAN IT

THE STUDIO PORTRAIT

My face is that of a young adolescent around twelve.
I looked like a movie starlet, or so I thought.

She is not asked to do the job. She is not capable. He has been taught to sew and iron by his mother who is a seamstress. He removes the detachable collar and cuffs, washes and irons them and sews them back on. He does this very angrily and very quickly and we are out the door. The effect of his tantrum hangs around, but this is what he is like and if we want to wrest pleasure from disaster we have to get happy quickly. I am always slow to do this, because I am like my father in all the bad ways a girl can be.

Sometimes my father and I were in the car alone. He would turn on talk radio, and then as now it was full of

My Father's Attitude toward Debts was Similar to His Feeling About speeding tickets. ~~His~~ He ignored them.

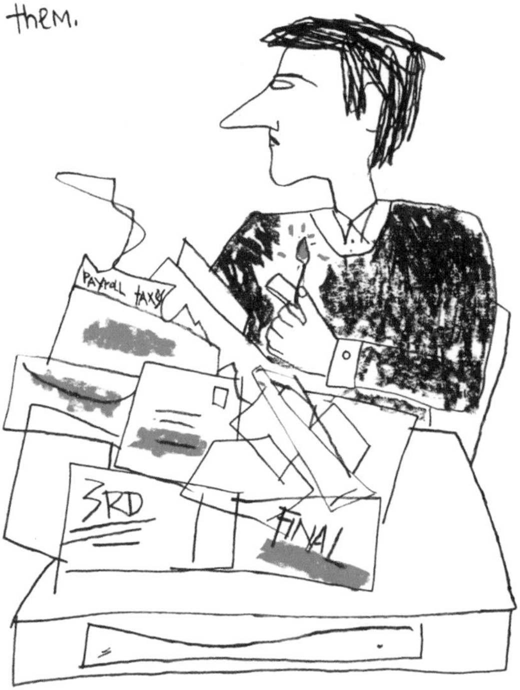
Payroll taxes
3RD
FINAL

angry, ranting right-wing conservatives. He loved listening. I hated it. Then and now I prefer to listen to people who agree with me. He had a different attitude. He said, "It's important to know what they're up to." I think this is a male trait, admirable like jumping into freezing cold lakes.

I remember that he carried a carton of milk in the car for his ulcers. I hoped what he did helped. Maybe he should have quit listening to right-wingers on the radio.

It shouldn't have come as any surprise to us that dad had not paid his taxes for some time. I was a child when the IRS came after him and garnished his salary. Interesting word, makes you think of tiny olives or thin slices of onion or crushed basil. I would wonder for years whether I had inherited his blatant disregard for government rules and regulations. Imagine my surprise when I realized I was more like my mother in this regard. I was terrified of the IRS and not only hired someone to keep track of my bill paying but an accountant to do my taxes.

At any rate, dad was in deep, so deep that he rated a visit at the house from an IRS agent. Oddly enough that agent was an old boyfriend of my mother's, the one who was a boxer, brother to her best friend Esther, and fated to marry my father's distant cousin from Kenosha, Clare. (She lived with us as well.) I don't know how my mother managed to get the old boyfriend, Sammy (yes, that was his name), to discuss unpaid taxes with Dad. I didn't know what the options were: jail time? A payment plan? The one that was offered was garnishment of wages.

DAD toLd Me

MISINFORMATION FROM MY FATHER

wHere's the rest of Me?

I was the only child in the neighborhood that knew what a capon was. Ca-pon: a castrated rooster raised for food. Of course my father taught me that. He loved outraging others by teaching his daughter to recite appalling information.

One of my father's more reasonable ideas about child rearing was that children should be allowed to experiment with forbidden things. If they were given a small amount of alcohol, they wouldn't be driven to excess and become alcholics. I don't know what this insight was based on. He occasionally poured us two little glasses of beer. I don't imagine it came from some little craft beer maker—probably it was Schlitz. We drank in the kitchen. I liked the taste of beer, but I didn't love it. I tried smoking because I knew it looked cool on girls, but it made me feel somewhat sick. Not terribly sick, but not worth developing a habit. Marijuana made me sleepy. So what did I like? Boys. Boys who seemed dangerous like James Dean, but bad boys didn't come in powder form and getting involved with them seemed difficult. I was shy.

My father also taught me not to be ashamed of my body. This was purely theoretical. When I rode home on the bus on a lovely summer day, wearing only my bathing suit, without shorts or shirt covering my body, he couldn't believe it. He was furious. I was puzzled and hurt.

Much later as an adult, I tried cocaine. Wonderful! The experience was wonderful. I was always attracted to speed. Speed made me loquacious, energetic, creative, able to leap tall buildings in a single bound. I loved talking uncontrollably. When cocaine became so wonderful that the amount that usually lasted my boyfriend and me a week, began running out before Sunday, we quit.

What are my happy memories as a family? As a family we listened to the radio lying on the floor in the living room. Sunday was a big day for stories. I loved the comedies. Jack Benny was my favorite. I learned timing from him. I adapted it to my cartoon strip. The long pause and then the surprise, worked in cartoons as well. Fred Allen, Fibber McGee and Molly's closet, with Molly yelling: "No! No! Mcgee don't open the closet!" followed by sounds of tons of junk tumbling out of the closet.

I loved *The Bickersons*. Each episode started out amicably with them getting ready for bed. (They slept in a double bed I'm sure.) But an argument would start almost immediately and it would never stop, it accelerated, it took up the whole show. I remember none of the topics, but I loved how the fight grew from some tiny disagreement: perhaps

DAD AND I ARe sitting IN the KitcHEN discussing oNe oF His more reasonABLe theories of cHiLd reAring...

see, the thing is KiDs Are curious, AND iF you MAke A big deAL out of drinking, it MAkes drinking too AttrActive AND LEADs to ALcoHoLisM.

Questions I WAS too young to Ask. WHAt About sex? CouLD I try A LittLe? How about drugs? * I'D NeveR heArd About drugs. MY FAtHeR HAD A record. ONe oF the pHrAses "KicKing the GoNG Around." I HAD NO iDeA WHAt it meANt, but oNce AgAiN I KNow it referred to sometHing dAngerous. AND NO MAN I KNew SMoKeD! WHY?

whether the window should be open a bit more or less or the curtains should stay open or be closed.

I loved the mysteries: *The Thin Man, The Shadow*. "Who knows what evil lurks in the hearts of men? The Shadow knows!"

Then Marie Jo's mother, Jenny (of "I will beat up my husband's girlfriend and then he will beat me up" fame), got a television set. So Marie Jo had a TV. I would have traded those family evenings and certainly, I would have traded my difficult father for a television set.

The White Mouse

MY FATHER NEEDED A PET

The story I heard was that my father was in high school and the summer break was approaching. His science class was home to a white mouse. What to do with the tiny creature over vacation? My father eagerly raised his hand. He would take "Hamlet" (I have named him) home. He didn't discuss this with his mother; as soon as she saw the mouse, she insisted it had to go!

I think that Jewish mothers spent most of their day cleaning and

I HAD LUNCH WITH 2 very OLD COUSINS OF MY FATHER'S.

too much HAIR → Sophie* Louise

we were the ONLY RELATIVES WITH A DOG.

-your FATHER took A WHITE mouse home FROM HIGH SCHOOL DURING SUMMER VACATION. HIS MOM GAVE it to US.

WOW! that EXPLAINS A lot. tell ME MORE.

* SopHie HAD A CANOPY bed... SCANDALOUS FOR AN OLD WOMAN! MY FATHER sister WAS DISDAINFUL.

36

AS SOON AS I ASKED FOR
Another story, they
Stopped Speaking

we're old.

— we can't remember.

cooking and looking after too many children. There was no room for a pet. And a mouse! A mouse! Really? Why not invite bubonic plague into the house? My father turned to the only relatives he knew who would consider accepting an animal into the house—his cousins Sophie and Louise. They were the only people in his family who had a pet, a dog. Yes, if you were so weird as to be a Jewish family and have a pet, it would have to be a dog.

They had lots of animals. We didn't have pets; we didn't eat fresh vegetables with exception of corn. We ate bacon, but never pork chops. The lore was my mother had a miscarriage after eating a pork chop.

One day when I was twelve my father came home with a little cage filled with Kleenex and a tiny animal the same color as the tissue. He presented the creature to me. It was a white mouse. It would be my pet.

I don't recall asking for a pet. I didn't know anyone who had a pet. I vaguely remember we once had a bird. I was allergic to it. I developed some kind of flu. I have no idea if it was connected to the bird, but the bird left. I would have liked a cat if I had known that a cat was a possibility.

I did not bond with the mouse. I am ashamed, but I didn't. Many times I would leave the top off the cage.

The mouse would scramble out and run through the house.

My mother had a flair for the dramatic. She must have been about thirty at the time because my sister wasn't born yet. She was young, but with the appearance of the mouse in our apartment, she aged overnight. She was bent over. I think she wore a shawl to increase the effect. She would lift each foot and look beneath it before taking a step to make sure there was not a mouse lurking on the floor waiting to trip her up.

The mouse couldn't compete with the drama. One day he disappeared. Between the ages of fifteen and thirty my father longed for that mouse. First one woman and then another took his pet away without a moment's thought. I think of how long he waited and how he was thwarted and I am sorry. He might have been a different man.

Eating Quickly

DIFFICULT FAMILY DINNERS

so we couldn't
read at the
table, and
there would
be no more
pie. WHAT
WAS the
Point?

Little Sister

_UH, UH.

My mother cooked dinner. I think her food was fine, nothing to complain about. What she did magnificently was pie, apple pie, a short-lived visit to Paradise. She said we ate too fast and the result of all her talent and all that work disappeared too quickly. She said she would make no more pie.

My father made marvelous potato pancakes—tiny, crispy, tender in the middle, with sour cream and applesauce.

After school I had onion sandwiches on white bread covered with chicken fat. The brand name of the chicken fat was Lady Aster. That's something to ponder. What Jewish wit thought that one up?

We were not allowed to read at the dinner table. Dad was the only one allowed to read. Did we even talk? Or did we madly rush through the meal so we could go somewhere and read?

tHE Needy BABy iNside my Father's HeArt.

The kitchen table Never Looked like that because My FATHeR ReAd At the tAble

He Kept Apricots iN His top dvAwer.

He HAD FAR-RANGING interests

BUILDING A STAIRCASE, Visiting other PLANets

the King

OUR ROGERS PARK APARTMENT
With Christmas tree.

There was no TV, but there was radio. *The Green Hornet, The Shadow, Mr. and Mrs. North,* Jack Benny, Fred Allen, *The Bickersons*—the radio was a feast.

Dad had a needy child inside him. One that had to have his own cache of apricots that he kept in a drawer in his bedroom. On the other hand he was the most imaginative and generous giver of Christmas gifts, ones that we couldn't possibly afford. Were they charged? Was a bad check given in payment for them?

On Christmas morning I awoke to an enormous Christmas tree, fully decorated in the near-empty living room of our Rogers Park apartment, the apartment we moved to after leaving Lawndale.

Many others left Lawndale for the suburbs but that was not in the cards for us. We moved further north in the city and to a larger apartment. Really a lovely big space with very little furniture, refinished floors, and clean white walls.

That Christmas, what space was not taken up by the tree was filled with presents for me. A dollhouse with miniature figures and furniture bought at the Museum of Science and Industry. A box full of paints and brushes and pads of paper. What did my sister and mother receive? I don't remember. My gifts took up all the space in my head.

My Sister

AND THE COAT HANGER

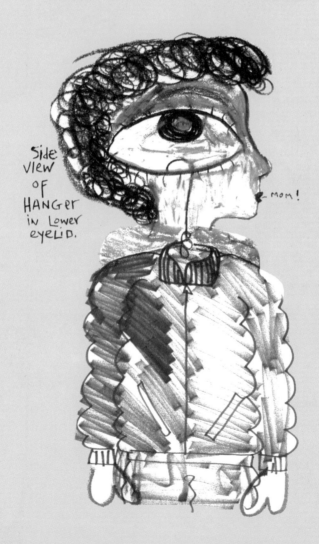

Side view of Hanger in Lower eyelid.

-mom!

My mother was always in the kitchen with a neighbor. They didn't work. They had no money. They took care of the children and drank coffee. Since no one had a pet, no dogs were walked. When their husbands were due to come home my mother's friends disappeared into their own kitchens and they all made dinner and perhaps put a bit of lipstick on.

SUIT HANGER

the SNOW SUIT AND HANGER LANDED IN HER EYE.

OH.

My sister was perhaps three years old with a head of brown curls. She was too short to reach her snowsuit on its hanger. She pulled the snowsuit down. The snowsuit and the hanger landed in her eye. She walked into the kitchen with the hanger and the snowsuit hanging from her eye. It was quiet, and then… my mother screamed!

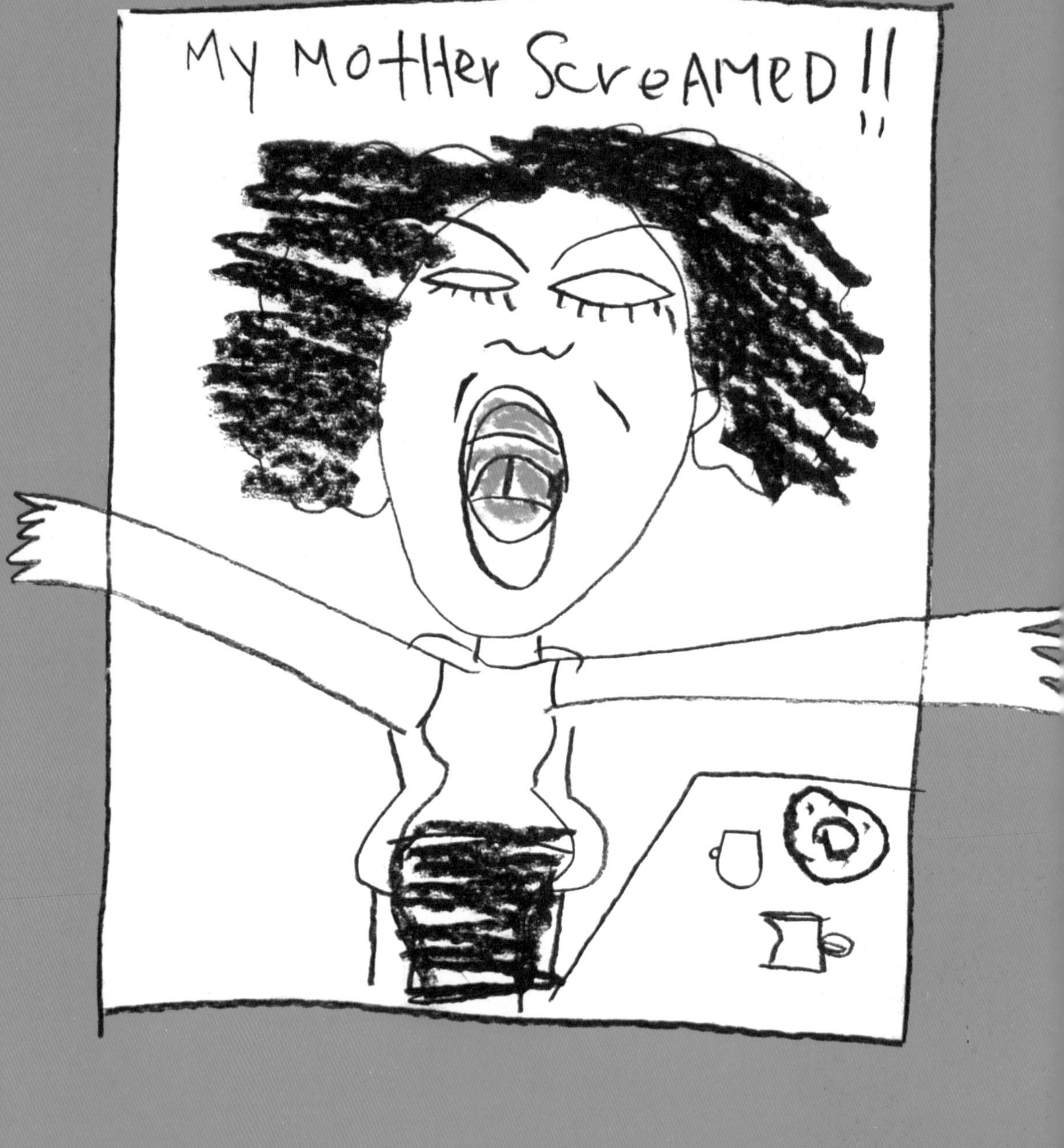
My Mother Screamed!!

After a moment, she reached over and calmly slipped the hanger out of my sister's eye.

Our lives were full of domestic catastrophes. They were handled, and things went back to normal.

I vowed I would never have children and I never did.

Harry

THE GANGSTER ON THE FIRST FLOOR

MY MOTHER AND I stare into each other's eyes as she teaches me the proper positioning of A drinking GLASS, so that it AMPLIFIES the voices of the couple below.

the special PLEASURE WAS in the CONTRAST between the prim demeanor of the WIFE AND Her behavior during AN ARGUEMENT.

STUPID CUNT!

LIMP Dick!

Harry loaned money to gamblers at high interest rates. He didn't have his own loan sharking business, he worked for others. He was just a guy working for more powerful guys. A guy who had a wife who wanted a full-length fur coat.

Harry needed to earn a little extra cash. His side business was magic tricks. I worked for Harry. At ten years old, I was also in need of cash.

My job was to pack the "nickel into dimes" trick. The nickels were shown to the mark, a crown (which held the dimes) was placed over the nickels. When you pressed on the top of the crown, it released the dimes.

I sat in his darkened dining room packing coins for hours. We toiled at the large dining room table. The blinds were drawn. Harry didn't talk much. We just pushed nickel-shaped coins into brass crowns. Harry gave me a ring once

I'M MAKING MONEY! I'M HAPPY.
Is this the LIFE I IMAGINED?
Shell
Ring
FLOOR

with a huge single zircon. I have it still. I keep it to remind me that a zircon will not turn into a diamond. No, that is not true. I keep it because one day I will open the little box and there will be a real diamond there.

Harry was a benign boss. There was nothing of the thug about him. His son, on the other hand, was a monster and once shot a sharpened pencil at my eye. Perhaps, had I been injured, I would have had a promising musical career as a blind violinist/pianist. This is a bit like my fantasy of discovering that my zircon has turned into a diamond.

MY FANTASY

*Blinded in childhood by
the brat downstairs,
she turns to the violin
and plays to packed
houses.*

The magic business didn't bring in enough. More money was needed to keep Florence calm. Harry started withholding cash from his bosses. Eventually they noticed. I can't image he was clever.

Tough guys worked Harry over with a two-by-four. He went to the doctor we all knew. Everyone in the building used Doctor Samuels. Harry was covered with blood. It was too good a story for the doctor to keep to himself. One day the entire family disappeared. It turned out they had gone to Washington D.C. They came back for a visit. No shame was attached to the episode.

Marilyn

THE PRINCESS ON THE TOP FLOOR

I WAS ALWAYS CRAZY ABOUT MEN*

* she said this to me years later when I treated her to lunch...

Hoping to bribe her into telling me about the nude photos. She was way too crafty for me. I HAD NOTHING TO TELL Her that WOULD pique Her interest.

SHE STARTED EARLY

Was it obvious, even in her baby buggy, that Marilyn would bring shame to her parents?

Princess Marilyn was the only daughter of Queen Bess and Mr. Grimzon. She was not a child; she was an adult, quite a tall woman who towered over her powerful parents.

They didn't need height. Her father didn't even need a first name. He was Mr. Grimzon, forever in the shadows, glimpsed on our way into Marilyn's room.

AND WHERE ARE MY boobies?

But WHAT iF they were SkeLetons uNDerNeath their robes?

they're Going to HAVE to WATCH Her Like A HAWK!

I Hope they KNOW A...

GOOD Doctor becAuse sHe's Going be PreGGers beFore SHe's 16.

Of course the "Royal Apartment" was at the very top of the Courtyard. The Queen and Princess Marilyn were always to be found there in the throes of dressing for a ball.

My mother and I were allowed to watch. We were suitably awestruck and they, in turn, accepted our admiration graciously.

My mother would ask Queen Bess impertinently, "Why aren't you dressed yet? Won't you be late?" and the Queen would reply: "We're all dressed underneath."

They wore robes over their underwear. We did not own robes. I didn't know any other people who wore robes.

The building we all lived in was a six-flat. The front apartments were bigger and more expensive. The owner

Yes,
Sweetie
we're
ALL
dressed
UNDerNeAtH.

of the building lived in one. All her furniture matched and all of it was blonde wood. We lived in the courtyard. We had one-bedroom apartments. Some of us slept in the dining rooms. I was one.

Marilyn was a maiden and therefore not allowed to live on her own. She would leave home only when safely married to a wealthy man. She was to be protected and coddled by her parents until such time as she would be passed on to an appropriate man and protected and coddled by him. If she couldn't have her own apartment, she could have her own chamber in their one-bedroom apartment. I don't know where her parents slept. To ask would have been rude.

Marilyn's bedroom had heavy, gray, silk shantung drapes that matched her bedspread and wall-to-wall carpeting and a vanity dresser with a huge mirror and perfume with atomizers in fancy bottles. Evening in Paris was in a cobalt blue bottle. I don't remember what it smelled like. I remember White Shoulders because my mother wore White Shoulders. Perhaps commoners weren't allowed Evening in Paris.

Once, late at night when I was sleeping in the dining room of our apartment, I heard sounds through the kitchen door… I heard Marilyn sobbing. A boyfriend had taken nude photos of her and was blackmailing her. The conversation was muffled and frustrating. I was afraid to stand too close to the door, afraid of being caught. I heard my father reassure Marilyn. He would take care of her problem. My father had a temper. He frightened my mother and me; surely he could take care of a sleazy boyfriend.

My mother is beyond my reach. I want to ask, "Where do you think the photos were taken? Was it Marilyn's room?" That would have been wonderfully ironic.

Everyone confided in my mother. Even I, who knew how untrustworthy she was, told her things. And my mother would have repeated everything that went on in the kitchen because it would have been a great story and she couldn't help but tell it.

MARILYN'S DRESSING TABLE

I'm sure that Marilyn's bedroom had a dressing table. Maybe it looked like this with a tube of bright red lipstick and a bottle of Evening in Paris eau de parfum.

My friend IrMA

BETTER THAN A REAL AUNT

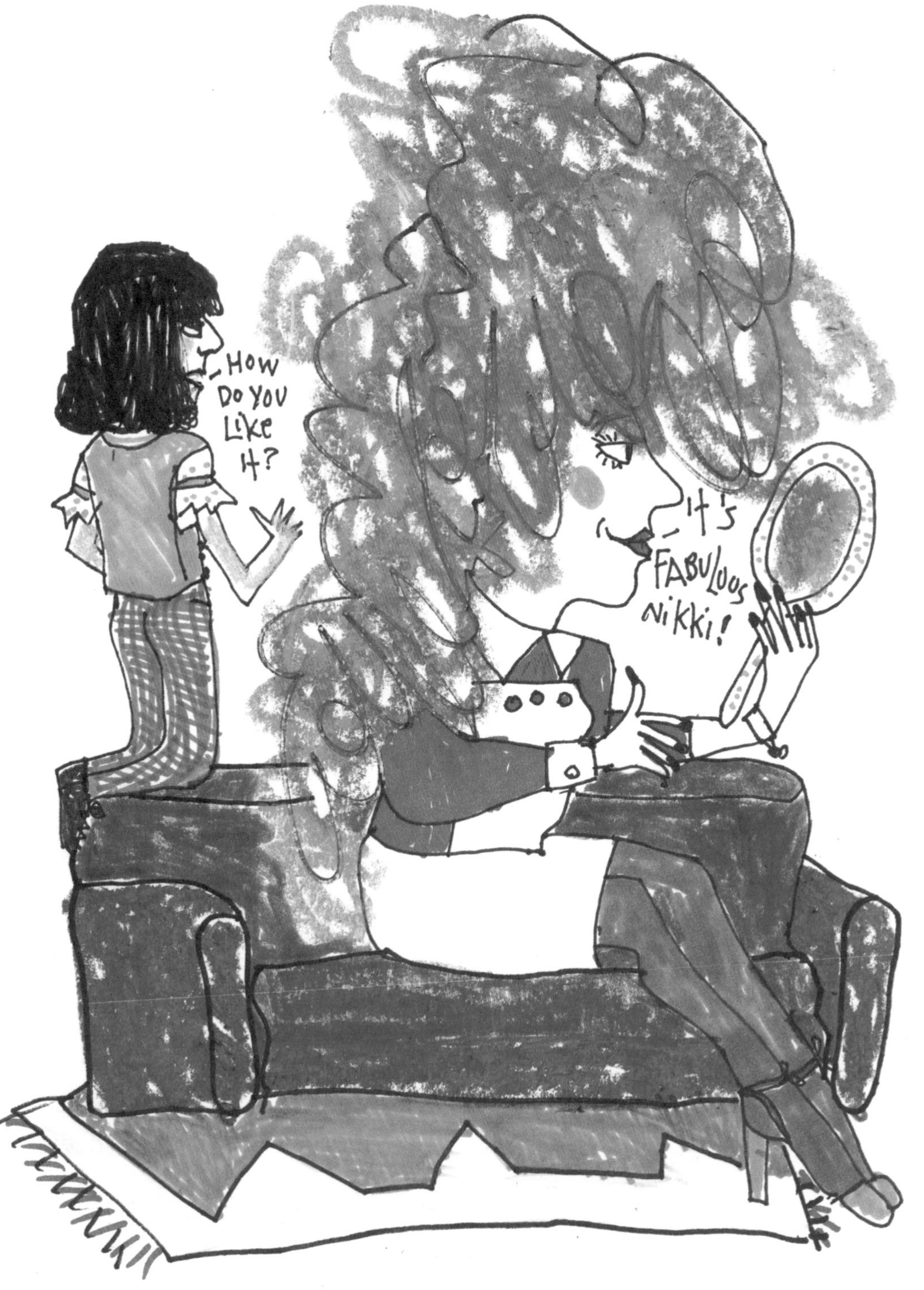
HOW DO YOU LIKE IT?
IT'S FABULOUS NIKKI!

don't remember how Irma came into my life. My mother's inner circle of friends were women she met as a teenager. They went door to door and sold magazine subscriptions. They dated boys who belonged to the same social club. They married those boys. They had children at the same time… all girls. They were always around, but Irma just suddenly appeared in my life with no background story, like my own personal fairy godmother.

Irma had heavy, dark blonde hair, we called it dishwater blonde. She often came to visit my mother after work. I imagined that she had a secretarial job, like her namesake on one of our favorite radio shows: *My Friend Irma*. She was unmarried. She lived with her younger brother Eliot, who was sickly. One night my parents told me that Eliot was in the hospital dying. Unmarried and alone, she picked me to be her niece, to be her favorite.

She would arrive at the door and I would be ready with a mirror and a comb and a little jar for her hairpins. As soon as she arrived she would sit on the couch in the living room and I would perch on the back of the couch and take the hairpins out of her hair. She had long hair that she wore rolled up on the sides, forties style. I took the pins out and her hair fell to her shoulders.

I began working my magic, turning an average-looking woman into a mess.

She pretended to enjoy it. She talked to me about my crushes. I had a crush on a boy named Jon in my 8th grade class. He was blond. She demeaned him if he ignored me. I have no idea whether he and I had anything to do with each other. I think it was all my fantasy of romance with a tall blond boy and had no basis in reality. Irma and I both took it seriously and discussed the details of my relationship in endless detail. During the week she would send me greeting cards and send personal notes asking about my life.

I don't think my mother ever sat with us. My mother was with her more flashy friends visiting psychics and chasing fire trucks for excitement. One day, Irma announced to my mother that she was getting married… married to an older man. I think this was surprising to my mother, who had written her off as an old maid who took care of a delicate younger brother. Her fiancé was Greek, perhaps owned a Greek restaurant. We had no idea how she met him. My mother cautioned her not to have sex the first night. I thought my mother was saying that Irma might be tired after the wedding celebration and would need to rest. Irma giggled at her, which I took to mean she would not be resting after the party.

The forties was the golden age of the ditzy blonde. Irma was an office worker who had a roommate, and a boyfriend she had been engaged to for fourteen years, one who never had a job. Irma tried to help everyone, but like Lucille Ball in *I Love Lucy,* she only succeeded in making everyone's life around her more complicated and zany.

My Friend Irma was introduced by a theme song written by Cole Porter. I quoted the lyrics in a memento I made after my mother died (shown below, my mother is second from the left). I gave copies to her friends. "When other friendships have been forgot, ours will still be hot..."

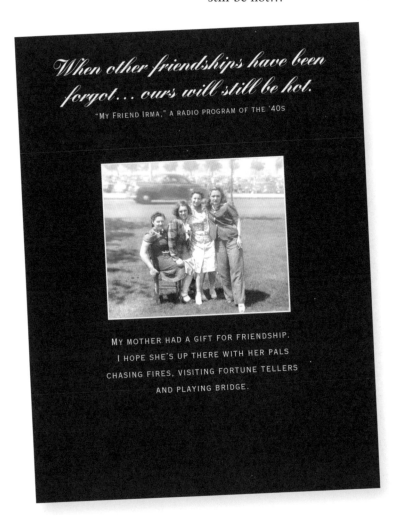

When other friendships have been forgot... ours will still be hot.
"MY FRIEND IRMA," A RADIO PROGRAM OF THE '40S

MY MOTHER HAD A GIFT FOR FRIENDSHIP.
I HOPE SHE'S UP THERE WITH HER PALS
CHASING FIRES, VISITING FORTUNE TELLERS
AND PLAYING BRIDGE.

A Healthy Diet

EATING ON CONGRESS STREET

I live in a neighborhood that has been revitalized by a gigantic new grocery store just across the street. It's huge and it sells only healthy food and cosmetics that have not been tested on animals. The cosmetics are so pure that you could eat them.

In the old neighborhood I don't recall women actually cooking. There were no delightful odors coming from anyone's kitchen. Women drank coffee all day and then rushed home to get some kind of meal on the table for the men.

The idea of vegetables as part of a balanced diet had not reached their consciousness. We were amazed that Jennie and Rosie (who were Italian, which explained the lettuce) served salads with their meals. They also served hot beef sandwiches for parties, bought at a local restaurant. The salads consisted of some kind of lettuce (Bibb?), torn and mixed with an oil-and-vinegar dressing. I don't recall tomatoes or artichokes or green peppers or any other vegetable being part of the salad. My mother didn't serve salad. Frozen vegetables hadn't come on the market yet and I don't think we ate canned vegetables, with the exception of creamed corn nibblets. We did eat canned fruit salad. When corn was in season we ate fresh corn, probably from my father's distant forays to the country in his Hudson.

WHY DOES MARIE JO HAVE SALAD FOR DINNER AND we don't?

BECAUSE LETTUCE doesn't come in A CAN.

We ate farmer's chop suey. Chop suey loomed large in our lives. We ate corned beef at delis and we ate chop suey at a restaurant. Farmer's chop suey was made with cucumbers, green onions, celery, and perhaps tomatoes (I realize I'm vague about tomatoes; I can't remember any color in our meals) tossed into a bowl of cottage cheese and sour cream with lots of salt.

My maternal grandmother, who did cook, was famous for her "Jewish Chop Suey," which was made wholly with canned Chinese vegetables (bok choy, bamboo shoots, celery, and unknown vegetables, pale yellow and too small to be identified) served with rice and soy sauce.

For an after-school snack I ate onion sandwiches on bread (Wonder Bread?) spread with chicken fat, from a jar labeled: "Lady Aster's Chicken Fat." Chicken fat is delicious. It tastes like melted butter and chicken and is very salty. Peanut butter and jelly didn't stand a chance.

We did not have a healthy diet. We put no stock in healthy food. My mother often said: "You have to eat a pound of dirt before you die," which explained why I could eat something I had dropped in the street after blowing on it. Swimming, of course, was as dangerous as bike riding, neither of which I have mastered. Many of the women smoked. I think those that didn't thought that the smell might be unattractive to men. The husbands of my mother's friends didn't smoke. No one eschewed smoking because of health issues. Smoking seemed glamorous and the sign of a woman who was a daring and alluring.

Marlene Dietrich made smoking a sign of sex and danger, smoke rising around her elegant face in the spotlight of a dark nightclub, with the male audience unable to take their eyes off her.

In the chapter "Eating Quickly," I may have given the impression that our family's diet was utterly devoid of pleasurable tastes except of course for after school snacks of "onion sandwiches made with chicken fat on Wonder Bread." Our diet on Congress Street was unmemorable but at our grandmother's houses, it was different.

At my maternal grandmother's we ate a wonderful meat dish called brisket; it was a beef roast. It was made with dried fruit (prunes and apricots), carrots, onions, and potatoes. It was cooked forever; "rare" anything was viewed with suspicion. Only hours of cooking made food safe against the plague. The flavors merged into something marvelous, both sweet and salty.

My father's talent for making potato pancakes was not revealed until my family moved into our own house in Glencoe. The pancakes were crispy on the outside and tender on the inside, served with applesauce and/or sour cream. He stayed in the kitchen and produced then one after another. As soon as they were done the crowd ate them so that they didn't spend a moment on a plate.

In high school, I remember going to a restaurant called Little Jacks every Friday. I ate the same lunch every week… a hot beef sandwich on white bread with mashed potatoes, covered in heavy brown gravy. A man I knew around my age, who owned several restaurants in Chicago, started his career by visiting every restaurant that served hot beef sandwiches to find the best. I'm sure he dreams of them still.

I was reminded of this today when I ordered a root beer float and shared it with a friend. I told her that my mother insisted that a root beer float could cure a broken leg. A slight exaggeration, but that float does seem to have magical properties.

I Envy Her

I WANT A NERVOUS BREAKDOWN, TOO

Marie Jo and her mother lived in a basement apartment in her grandfather's building. The apartment was dark with a low ceiling. There was a door that led to the back of the basement, but it was never open when I was there.

But Marie Jo's family had a television set. No one else did. My mother insisted that it was poor compensation for not having a father who lived with them. I was not so sure. In fact I would have traded my difficult father for that television in a minute.

Then Marie Jo had a nervous breakdown. The adults called it that. I knew that she stayed in her mother's double bed for a long time. She didn't get up, she didn't go out. I think she groaned occasionally. Maybe she had involuntary spasms. I think she was served meals in bed.

How could I compete with a nervous breakdown? She was Catholic. How could I compete with a religion that had such embellishments and so many rules? In church, she knew when to stand up and when to sit down and she put a wafer in her mouth and took a sip of wine from a silver chalice. This is an exaggeration: I think it was a plastic cup. She wore a uniform to school. What a boring childhood I had! I think I joined the Girl Scouts because of uniform envy.

I HAD CHICKEN
POX

MARIE JO
had something
More Mysterious,
Perhaps more
Spiritual ...A
crisis of the
SOUL...

A Nervous
BREAKdown!

I HAD CHICKEN
POX

One of Marie Jo's relatives suggested that she should be slapped and that would cure her nervous breakdown. I was terrified at the idea that someone would slap her, but it didn't happen. Eventually she just got up.*

All I had was chicken pox. I picked off the last scab so that I could go out with my friends. I have a tiny scar on my right temple. Big deal.

Oh, and another thing Marie Jo had were copies of *Tales from the Crypt*. I sneaked a peek at one, but I regretted

---

* *A friend asked: "What were Marie Jo's symptoms?" I realized I really didn't know. Parents didn't discuss diseases that were not mumps or measles in front of children. I think it was taken for granted that all boys had Attention Deficit Disorder, although it was not called that.*

Today I looked up mental illness in children, and something struck a chord: Phobias. I think Marie Jo was afraid to leave the safety of her mother's bed, afraid to leave the house. I remember that she complained of pains in her arms and legs, but I think the uneasy atmosphere, both financial and emotional gave her a reason to cling to the safety of her mother's bed and of the apartment.

I told a friend this story for the first time and she said: "When I was a child, I was phobic about cleanliness. I took a damp washcloth to bed so I could keep my hands clean at night."

I HAD CHICKEN POX. It's ALMOST GONE.

THERE'S ONLY ONE SCAB LEFT. MY MOTHER SAYS I CAN'T GO OUT WITH MY FRIENDS UNTIL THE SCAB FALLS OFF.

NIKKI, DID YOU PICK OFF THAT SCAB?

MOM! IT WAS A MIRACLE* IT FELL OFF BY ITSELF!

* IF HE COULD PART THE RED SEA, COULDN'T HE MANAGE SMALLER MIRACLES? IS OUR GOD SOME KIND OF SNOB?

it. The image of a young handsome boy blinded by jealous rivals was horrible, but the image of the revenge that the circus people took on the perpetrators lasted my whole life. Circus people. Of course! Think of the half-man half-woman and the fat lady and the freaks that ate live chickens on the midway.

My mother didn't allow me to buy comic books—not because of nightmares that would last a lifetime—but because they cost ten cents and you only read them once. I knew a girl who bought herself a condo with her comic collection. Summer clothes were frowned upon for the same reason. Summer was such a short season that there was no point buying summer clothes. This changed when I got older. My mother was working and making money and she liked to dress me up in expensive, sophisticated clothing that my small frame was just the right size for. I got into it. It was like a drug. When I started to make money drawing cartoons, I developed a heavy habit at a store that was so expensive they didn't have a sign. If you didn't know where they were, you didn't deserve to shop there.

The Chocolate Banana

SEX AND THE GARDEN

WE HAD A FENCED IN AREA behind the APARTMENT. IT WAS FULL OF GARBAGE.

I CAN CLEAN this UP AND TURN it into A BEAUTIFUL GARDEN.

Outside our section of the building was a wrought iron arch with the legend 3914 W. Congress worked into it. There were no plants anywhere outside.

The only color in the neighborhood was the lush zinnia garden grown by Jenny's Italian father-in-law. I wanted a garden. The only land available was at the back of our building. It was full of broken glass and stones. I worked tirelessly to clear it, but there was no sun and I don't recall getting any help or any advice. I didn't understand that it was necessary to plant in order for plants to grow. I thought once the yard was clean, flowers were automatic. A year later and wiser, I was so hungry for flowers that I planted some seeds on the back porch in the window box. There was no sun there either. I would visit the seeds quite often until my father in desperation bought some cut flowers and stuck them in the box. I was not amused.

I know as much about sex as I do about growing a garden.

I visit the dictionary in front of my classroom most mornings looking for something about sex. Some definition that will make it all clear. I think: "I will know it when I see it."

The family next door has a television set. Jenny is now my mother's best friend in the neighborhood. Marie Jo, her daughter, is mine. My family is invited

to watch Dean Martin and Jerry Lewis on *The Ed Sullivan Show*. Afterwards Jenny puts a record on the turntable. It plays one record at a time. I remember the song. It went, "He's got the cutest little dinghy in the Navy." It's a catchy tune. I have no idea what it means, but I know it is sex.

Another time I am in the neighborhood candy store. I ask to buy a chocolate-covered banana. A tough looking older girl who I don't know taunts me: "Doesn't your father have one?" I don't know what she's asking, but I know it's "sex."

The neighbors next door were Catholic. Jenny had three children. Marie Jo, Barbara Jean, and Little Anthony. Her husband, Big Anthony did not live with them. I understood that because they were Catholic, they couldn't get divorced. My mother said she wouldn't divorce my father because she didn't want me to have a stepfather. Why not? A stepfather was an unknown commodity—why not take a chance?

Jenny beat up her husband's girlfriend and then Jenny's husband beat her up. She appeared in a sleeveless summer dress with bruises on her arms. She didn't try to cover her bruises. There was something honorable in getting them and showing them. My mother just quietly injured herself with kitchen accidents and miscarriages.

I was always visiting Marie Jo's church and the priest was friendly to me. I think he thought I was convert material. Had he ever met my father? Marie Jo told me that because she was Catholic she had to wear a shift when she took a bath, so that she wouldn't look at her naked body and become fixated on it. Nobody cared how long I stayed in the tub. I wished that I had strictures that gave my life more drama.

Minnie

Jenny

ant. bruises on ARMS (UPPER)

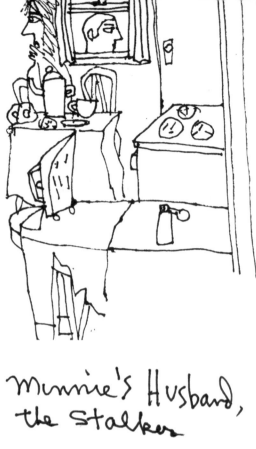

Minnie's Husband, the Stalker

US Army

The neighborhood stalker, who we were warned about, also lived in the greystone next door and was married to Minnie, Jenny's sister-in-law. He was rumored to approach young girls and goose them. (What did he really do? I have no idea.) We were careful to look around when we were on the street alone. The explanation for his behavior was that something had happened to him in the war. Then we stopped hearing about him. He was gone.

on the Bus

UNWHOLESOME SPORTS

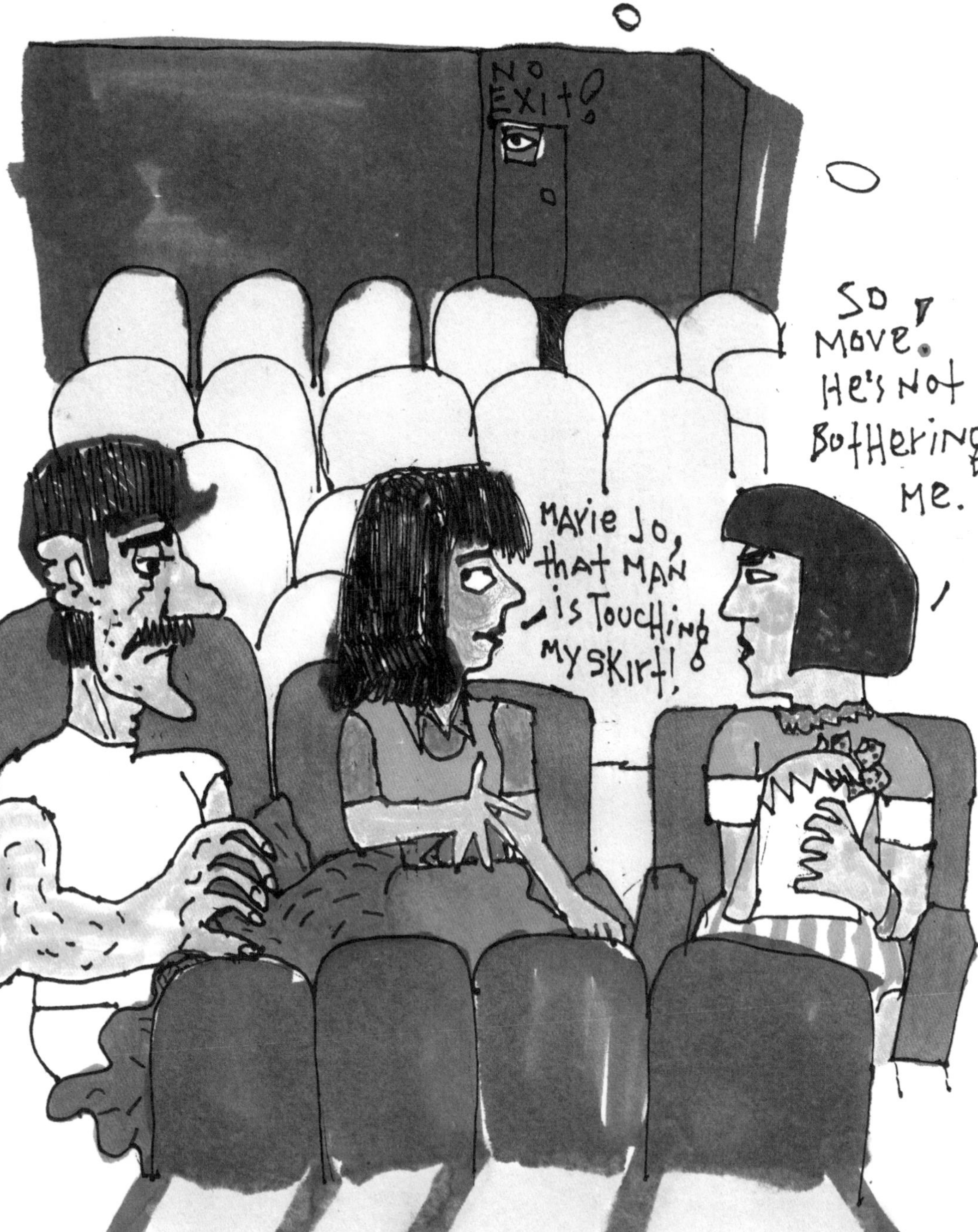
NO EXIT!
MArie Jo, that MAN is TouCHing MY SKirt!
So Move! He's Not Bothering Me.

ur neighborhood was considered perfectly safe for little girls; anything we wanted to do during the day was fine. We didn't leave the house after dinner. Before dinner we could do anything, go anywhere. We went shopping in the neighborhood, we took the bus downtown.

We went downtown to the movies ourselves. Sometimes I went alone.

Often I'd be sitting on a double seat on the bus happily looking out the window and suddenly a man would sit down next to me and begin to gyrate in his seat, his hands in his pockets.

I would give him a mean look. He would look away innocently, perhaps whistling a happy tune. Sometimes I would move to another seat. He would not follow me. No one seemed to care and remark on what he was obviously doing. "Playing Pocket Pool," said my father. He did not forbid me to ride on the bus nor did he seem to think I needed any extra instruction to protect myself from these men.

Marie Jo and her little sister Barbara Jean and I went to a movie one Saturday. Robert Mitchum had tattoos on his right and left hand; when he threaded his fingers together: they spelled out "Love and Hate." He was an evil preacher and he was single-mindedly looking for a little girl who had a doll stuffed with money.

WHY ARE MEN SO UNCOMFORTABLE WHEN WOMEN DON'T SMILE?*

Little Girl you'D be So much prettier IF YOU'D SMILE.

AND YOU'D Be better looking with A bAg over your head

But you don't HEAR me GIVING out ADVICE.

*the term: "resting bitcH Face" WAS NOT COINED WHEN I WAS A CHILD, but the sentiment Existed even then.

Fabulous! I was scared out of my mind. Perfect. I was intent on the movie, so it was a while until I noticed that edges of my wide skirt were moving back and forth as if there was a gentle breeze in the theatre.

"Marie Jo," I hissed, "the man next to me is moving my skirt." She looked at me disdainfully. "We're not changing our seats!" So I changed seats alone and went to the back of the theater.

Here again, there was a limit to what a pervert would attempt on a bus or in a movie theater. He stayed in his seat, perhaps playing pocket pool or making

waves in someone else's poodle skirt.

I became a danger to myself and a temptation to others, when I hit my early teens. One summer day I went to North Avenue Beach with friends and I rode home on the bus in only my uncovered bathing suit. No top, no shorts.

My father was outraged: "You rode on the bus like that?" I had no idea that there was any shame connected with my body. I was not in danger from any pervert I ran into. My body in a swimsuit was the danger. My father couldn't explain it to me. He was apoplectic.

If I returned late from a date my father would shout from the darkened bedroom: "You'll never be allowed out again." Now I imagine that my mother was lying next to him all night feeding him her fears: "Nikki's been attacked, raped, Italian boys on stolen rusty bikes gang-raped her, she's lying in the street bleeding to death, she's been kidnapped, she's lying bound and gagged in one of those partially torn-down buildings across the street." (I was not allowed to cross the street any longer because of the expressway construction.)

Wandering perverts were no danger, but my new breasts and the idea that I had gotten from my father that there was nothing shameful about my body would soon lead me into trouble. My father's discussions on physical freedom were purely intellectual. He didn't really mean it.

I dREAM of Badges

BUT ONLY EARNED ONE

I dreamt that I slept under a quilt covered with girl scout badges I earned.

the truth was that I had earned just ONE! A badge for cooking.

My troop made cream puffs. the main ingredient was canned fruit cocktail, drained and stuffed into ready-made cream puff shells.

All girls long to dress up. I wanted to wear a uniform. Catholic girls wore uniforms; nuns wore elaborate outfits with hats like huge swallows. Since I was a Jewish girl, the daughter of a rabid atheist, I decided to join the Girl Scouts. Our Girl Scout troop met at the Golden Dome in the Garfield Park Fieldhouse. It was very grand inside with intricate mosaics and topped by a fabulous golden dome.

I didn't start out as a Brownie. I was a Girl Scout from the get-go. No other kid from my block was a Girl Scout. But the more elite parts of the neighborhood had Girl Scouts, Jewish Girl Scouts. We met in living rooms and kitchens and did Girl Scout things. There was very little of the outdoors in our version of scouting.

This sanitized style of camping took place in the grown ups' apartments. It satisfied the demands of Jewish parents, the biggest one being utter safety. To insure the level of safety necessary, there could be no actual camping—the kind where your feet touch the earth—no contact with the elements, with trees, with rabbits, or with bodies of water not constrained by concrete and protected by railings. What kind of campgrounds would be reassuring enough for over-protective parents and campers? Hard to imagine.

Campers slept on the ground in tents. They cooked hot dogs over fires they built themselves. They swam, they canoed. They jumped off splinter-ridden wooden platforms. They slept in rooms that resembled army barracks, in narrow uncomfortable bunk beds, with itchy covers and flat mattresses. There were bugs leaping, flying, crawling. Bugs crowded around the pathetic light in the ceiling.

What did campers eat? "S'mores," whatever that was. Until I was twenty and got my first job as a camp counselor, I had no idea what an out-of-town camp looked like.

In some unspoken way it was made clear to me that my parents didn't really want me to go to camp. I think they didn't have the money to send me off for two weeks in the country, and besides, it scared my mother to death. I sensed that my mother wanted me to believe that camp is where unwanted children are sent. I did. I said so to my mother, and with a great sigh of relief my mother said, "Nikki doesn't want to go to camp," and the subject was closed.

Most of all, what I wanted from Girl Scouts was a uniform covered with the many brightly colored badges I had earned. My dream was never in the cards. I think I got a cooking badge. That was it and I was lucky to get it. We baked in someone's mother's kitchen. We made cream puffs. The cream puffs were premade. We had fruit cocktail in

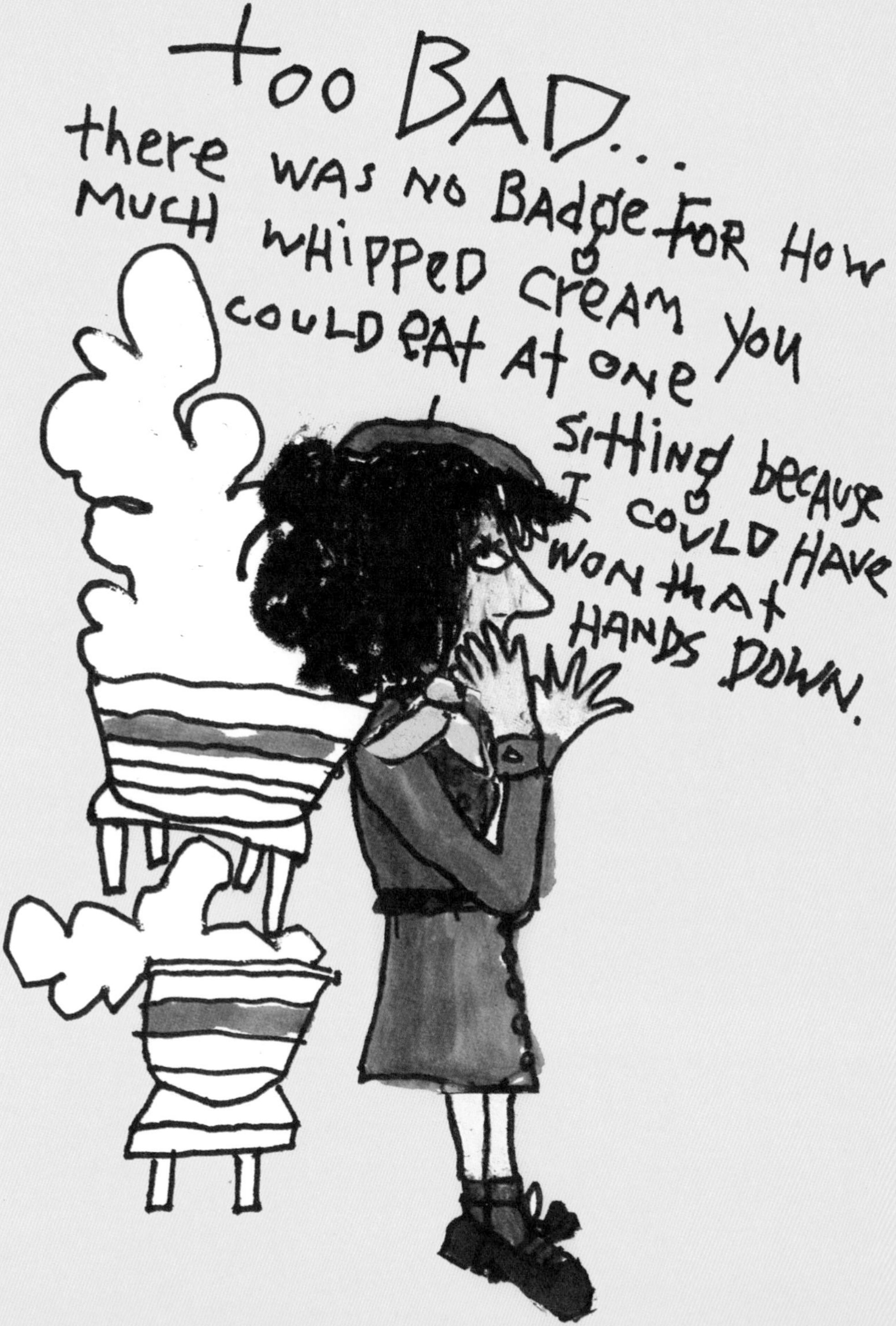
too BAD...
there WAS NO BAdge FOR How
MUCH WHIPPED cream you
could eat at one
sitting because
I could have
won that
HANDS DOWN.

CANNED FRUIT COCKTAIL

The most important ingredient of the cream puffs that earned me my only Girl Scout badge.

a can. We drained the syrup so the cream puffs weren't soggy. We stuffed the fruit cocktail into the puffs, arranged them on a pretty serving plate, and squirted whipped cream on top. And voila! Dessert.

I have never strayed far from that model in my culinary efforts. I know delicious stuff when I see it. I can decorate a table with cut-up paper and miniature food and miniature people. I think about learning to cook all the time. I have taken cooking lessons. I took Chinese cooking lessons. I took extensive notes, but when one of the other students borrowed my notes she pronounced them illegible. I took cake decorating. When I was married I learned how to cook a few Hungarian dishes. I can make them. Really. Don't worry, they are quite good. They rely heavily on sauerkraut, lots of meat, rice, sour cream, and you cook them forever and they last until you are heartily sick of them.

Aside from never ever leaving my neighborhood for away camp, I was an enthusiastic Girl Scout. I'm sure I sold Girl Scout cookies to all the neighbors and all my relatives and people who lived in the courtyard and strangers as well.

There was a stage in the fieldhouse. A no-frills stage. I wrote one-person shows and performed them on that stage. I don't know if I had an audience. I certainly didn't discuss it with anyone. I also put on plays in the old neighborhood on Congress Street in a deserted backyard. I had an old book of Shakespeare. I fed the kids their lines and they said them.

Putting on plays in the backyard did not lead me to a life as a playwright or an actress. Somehow I was derailed and became a cartoonist.

the WAY others Lived

EATING SPAGHETTIOS OUT OF THE CAN

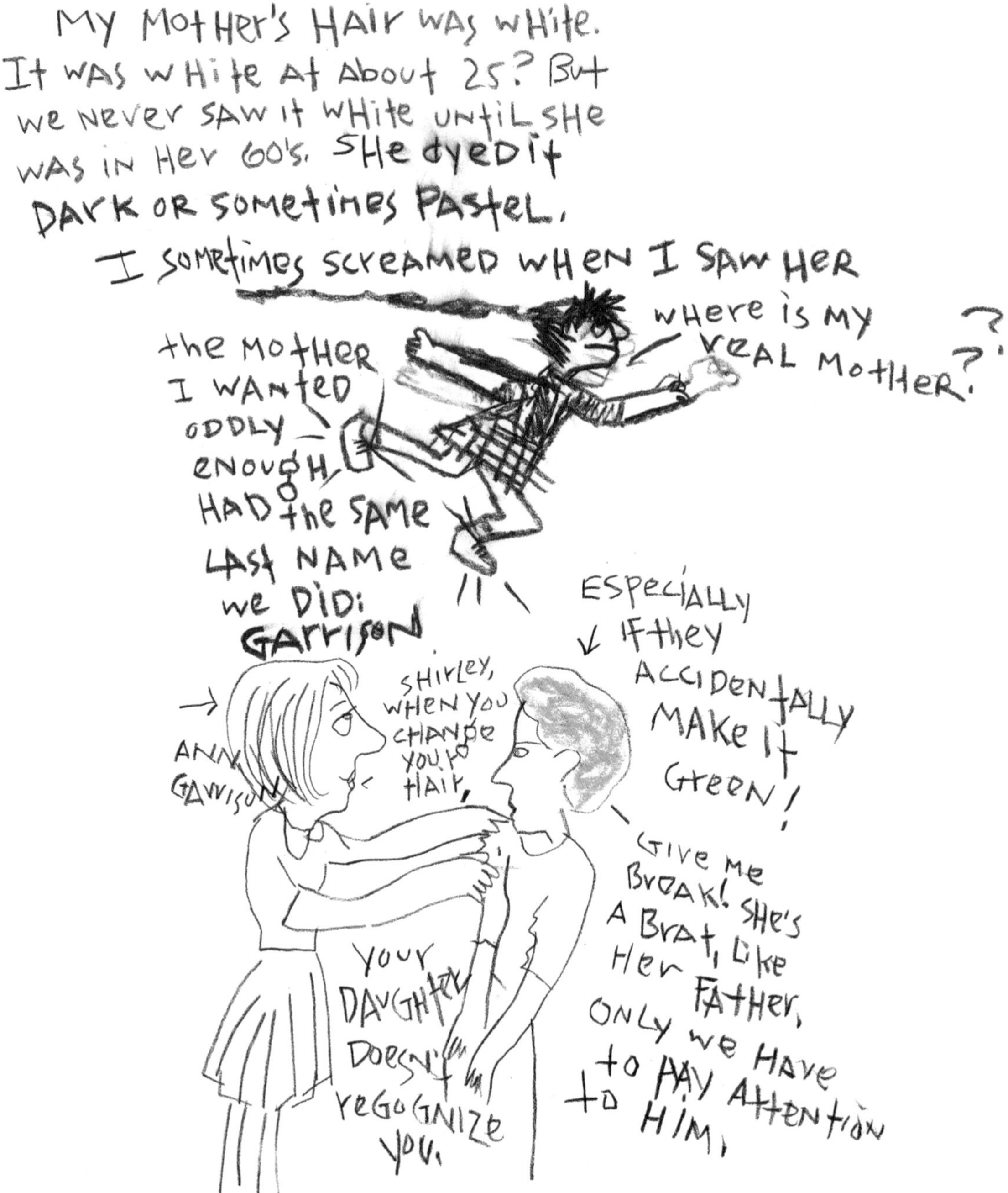
My Mother's Hair was white.
It was white at about 25? But
we never saw it white until she
was in Her 60's. She dyed it
dark or sometimes pastel.
I sometimes screamed when I saw her
where is my real mother?
the mother I wanted oddly enough had the same last name we did: Garrison
Especially if they accidentally make it Green!
Shirley, when you change you(r) hair,
Ann Garrison
your daughter doesn't regognize you.
Give me Break! She's a Brat, like Her Father, only we have to pay attention to Him.

I'm having dinner at a school friend's house—Ann Garrison, who lives on Jackson Blvd. Her family has the same last name as mine. Ann's mother keeps a drawer full of costumes for us. We can go into that drawer at any time and pretend to be anything. Her mother is an artist. Does that explain it? Do I even know what an artist is? No, I don't.

I'm hanging out in the living room with Ann's mother and Ann. We're waiting for my mother to come back from the beauty shop.

My mother arrives and her hair is an odd green color. I begin to scream hysterically, "Where is my real mother?" and throw myself around the room. Ann's mother says calmly to my mother, who is looking sad and puzzled, "Nikki doesn't recognize you because your hair is a different color. She doesn't know that you're her mother, and she's frightened." Ann's mother knows everything and she is kind and generous. I so wish she was my mother.

I am invited to a school friend's birthday party. His name is Richard. He also lives on Jackson Blvd. The people on Jackson Blvd. are different.

It's only now that I realize that the difference is class—education and money. These people are educated. They live differently than we do. We are poorish and lower middle class. My father works at a job that is interchangeable with any other job he's ever had. My mother doesn't work.

But today we kids are seated at a large dining room table. The dining room is not someone's bedroom like ours is. It is a single-purpose room.

A small group of Richard's schoolmates are seated around a huge table covered with a white cloth. The cloth is large enough to cover the entire table. Richard's mother greets us and we are seated. Do we have place cards? She moves around the table, friendly and assured, taking individual photos of us.

We have never been individually photographed, we have never been singled out. We are dazed. In a few minutes she returns with envelopes. Our names are written on the envelopes. We are told that our photos are inside. So fast. How could it happen so fast?

I open my envelope and inside is a postcard, a reproduction of a painting. Later I realize it's Renoir, a painting of a lovely young woman with rosy cheeks and dark hair.

I realize this girl is me. Richard's mother thinks I look like this young woman. I am stunned. Lots of things have happened to me in a lifetime, but none so perfect as that moment.

I Heard You!

HURTFUL REMARKS

remember going to the corner store for Wonder Bread. We were always admonished by our mothers not to squeeze the bread. If you squeezed it, it became a tiny wad and could not be used to make sandwiches or anything but spitballs.

A boy I recognize vaguely from school stands very close to me and hisses: "You killed Jesus." I was of course frightened of him, his size and intensity, but I had been raised by an atheist and felt no guilt about something I didn't think existed, like God. I was too young to say: "Really, the Jews killed Jesus, all of us? Did you ever see us in a room together trying to agree on anything?"

My experience of anti-Semitism was very limited as a child. We lived in a mainly Italian neighborhood, but the building we lived in was completely Jewish.

But I did hear slurs at neighborhood parties. I was a kid. I looked like all the other dark-haired kids and occasionally someone in the group would say someone "jewed" him down. "Jews have all the money, there are no poor Jews, Jews stick together." I could feel the remark coming. I was on the alert. Here is a group of people who are among their own kind. Why should they be careful about what they say? Suddenly the remark is made and I feel the spotlight

this WAS A MOM
It WAS At this co
cHrist!" "WHat's
I WAS ScAreD of
biG! He was so
For A joke. I wa
Direction were

D Pop grocery store when I was a kid.
r that a boy confronted me. "Jews killed
me," I thought. "I'm an Aetheist."
rse, because he was a boy and
nse. it was not the moment
-ung. my abilities in that

YOU KILLED CHRIST! WHAT'S IT TO ME?

on me. I am frozen and yet highly alert, my mind is working at top speed.

The idea that I might let the remark pass is certainly tempting, but not an option. I have a duty to all those Jews who died in the camps.

I say: "I'm Jewish." There is a terrible silence. These are nice people. I know them all. They are ashamed. They apologize. They say they didn't know. They didn't mean it.

I feel the urge to reassure them that I will forgive them and that I am not permanently injured.

The moment passes, everyone starts laughing and talking again, but I could ruin it all in a minute.

In the Deli

TROUBLE WITH DAD'S PARTNERS

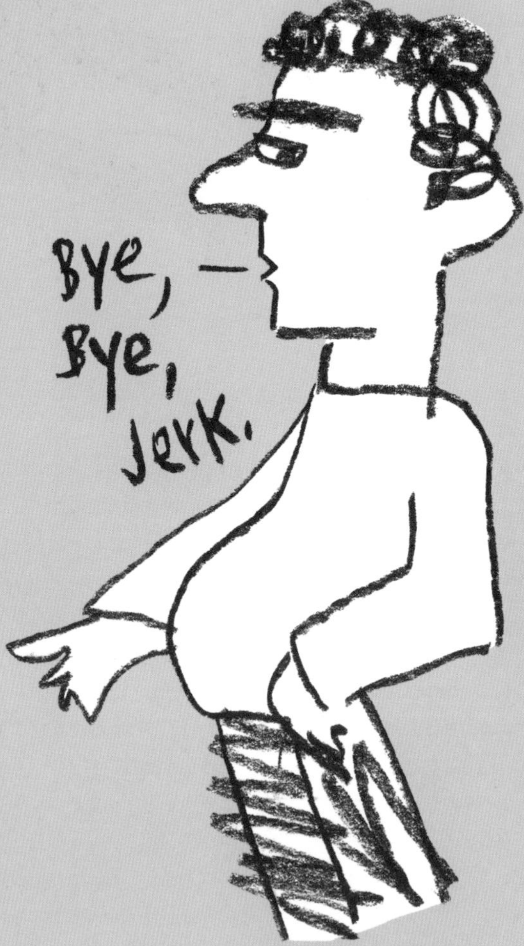
Bye,
Bye,
Jerk.

My father did not play well with others. I have that in my DNA. We like to start our own business and never, if we can help it, work for anyone else. If working for someone else is unavoidable, we try to get fired as soon as possible.

My father had a number of unsuccessful business ventures. Sometimes he had a partner. These partners didn't last. My father opened a small restaurant, the Pine House Deli. We all worked there. My sister worked in utero. His partner walked out before the restaurant even opened.

I peeled potatoes, and my mother was a waitress. I also cleared the counter, but I was impatient and often I would clear the counter before the customer was finished, which led to threats and hurt feelings. ("I'll just take these things out of your way." Customer: "I wasn't finished. Do you know what I did to the last waitress that did that?" "What?" Customer: "I shot her." "Oh." "She's dead.")

One of the regulars at the Pine House Deli would come in for coffee at odd times. He played the jukebox and seemed to have all the time in the world

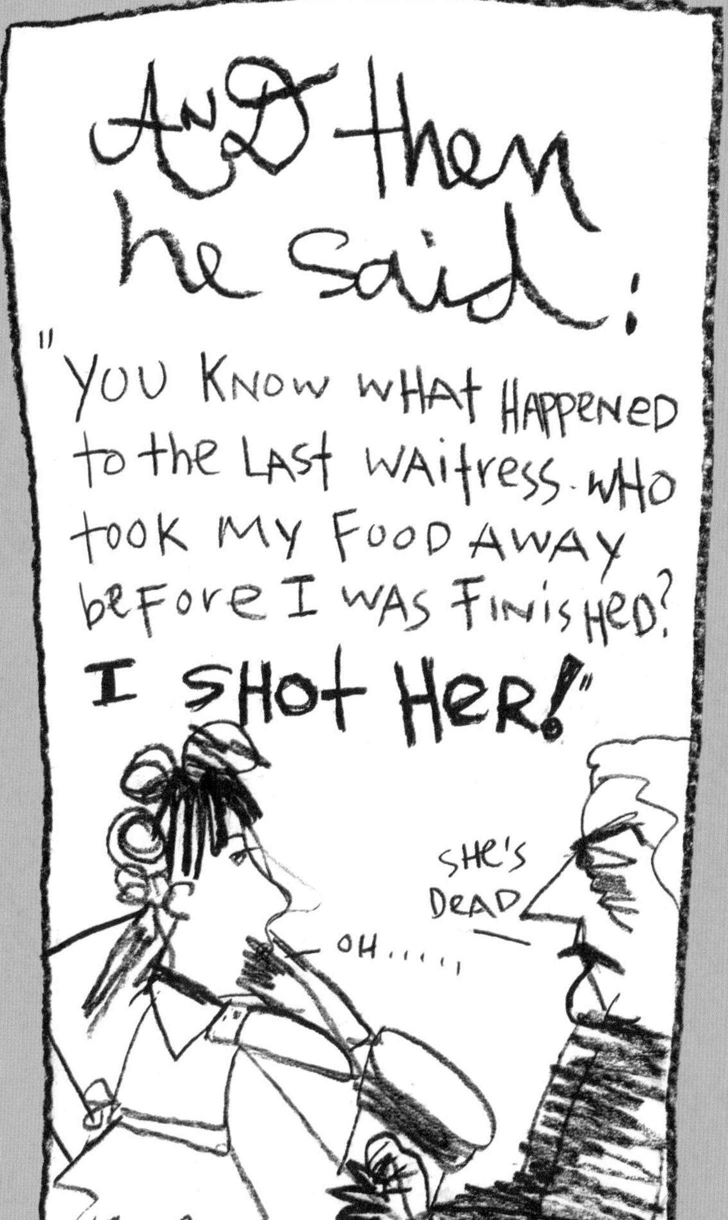
AND then he said:
"YOU KNOW WHAT HAPPENED to the LAST WAItress. WHO took MY FOOD AWAY before I WAS FINISHED?
I SHOT HER!"
SHE'S DEAD
OH.....

to stare into his coffee cup. I found out that he was a freelance book illustrator. I had no idea that was a job. I was hooked. It was the conversation that changed my life.

I think that led to me becoming a cartoonist. I wanted to be a cartoonist and drink coffee with others who seemed to have no regular jobs, no place to be.

Because my mother worked at the deli, I ate lunch at my Aunt Belle's house. She lived right across from my grammar school: Delano. Named after Franklin Delano Roosevelt.

THE CONVERSATION THAT CHANGED MY LIFE

Lunch at Aunt Belle's

WITH MY COUSIN'S COMIC BOOKS

Not all of life happened on Congress Street. Now my mother worked every day in my father's restaurant, the Pine House Deli. Every day I ate lunch at my Aunt Belle's house. My cousin was there. He tormented me in a special way. He would intently read his comic book and suddenly he would break out in a hideous voice and announce, "I'm coming to get you! I'm on the first step."

I would scream. The comic book was one of those *Tales from the Crypt* comics that terrified me. It was the cover that did it. I never looked inside one. Okay, I looked at one at Marie Jo's house.

COMICS

I was not allowed to read comics. I don't think it was their content. It was because they cost ten cents and you only read them once. This applied to summer clothes as well, because summer is such a short season. Mostly I got secondhand summer clothes. They were mailed in a box. The anticipation of a surprise made me high as a kite. Often they didn't fit me. I was too small, too skinny. I was disappointed every time.

A handsome, wholesome young man was in love with a carnival girl. The others hated him. Don't know why. They decided to blind him. Don't remember how.

Afterward, he was revenged! Not sure by whom, but they tied and gagged the miscreants in a hollow log and the young man was invited to saw into the log. He did. And lived happily ever after with the blonde girl.

Every kid threatened his tormenter: "I'm telling." And every parent said: "Don't make me come in there."

It's All My Fault!

I DIDN'T DO MY PART

I WAS — A Shirker.

IN the OLD NEIGHBORHOOD —there's A WAR ON

you MUST collect NewsPAPers

I collect NewspAPers, but MY ♥ isn't in it!

I want to help the WAr EFFORT!

I collect ONLY 3 Sheets of PAPER.... SHAME ON YOU !!

BECAUSE of Me, w

DELANO SCH

I'm very sorry!

it's ALL YOUR FAULT!

At school we were asked to collect old newspapers for the war effort. I had no idea how this would help us to defeat Nazis, so I'm afraid I approached the assignment with little enthusiasm. In a state of last-minute desperation, when the drive was over, I managed to collect three or four pages.

I looked around the schoolyard and saw children with little red wagons packed with tied up newspaper. I was embarrassed and ashamed, but it was too late!

I did blame my lackluster compliance on the fact that I did not own a little red wagon. I can't imagine my mother would have understood a need for a girl to own a little red wagon. What would I carry in it? If I went to the corner grocery store I bought a loaf of Wonder Bread. I didn't need a wagon for that.

Aunt Belle's Lamps

THEY FILLED MY DREAMS

My aunt had a table lamp on in her living room on Adams Street. The base of the lamp was a high-gloss ceramic figure of a dancing girl. The idea that she might be a prostitute or a sex slave didn't spoil anyone's appreciation of the beauty of the lamp. Her dress was skintight and her bodice was plunging. I wanted that lamp.

But at six or seven I couldn't make a case for my ownership of it, and I slept in the dining room and it would have looked out of place.

I drew that lamp over and over. I have an image of a cat knocking over a variation of that lamp. Almost every cartoon strip I did was crowded with lamps.

Years later when my aunt was very old, I called her to see if she still had the lamp. I knew it wasn't possible, but I thought I would give it a try.

Still kind and dutiful, she went into her living room to find it, with me shouting over the phone: "It's not there. It was there when you lived on Adams Street. She came back, to report sadly, "I can't find it."

All of Sylvia's table lamps and the upholstery on her couches and the wallpaper patterns originated on Congress Street in our living room or on Adams Street in my aunt's living room.

Marlene

MY FRIEND TWO HOUSES DOWN

She means the WORLD to me.

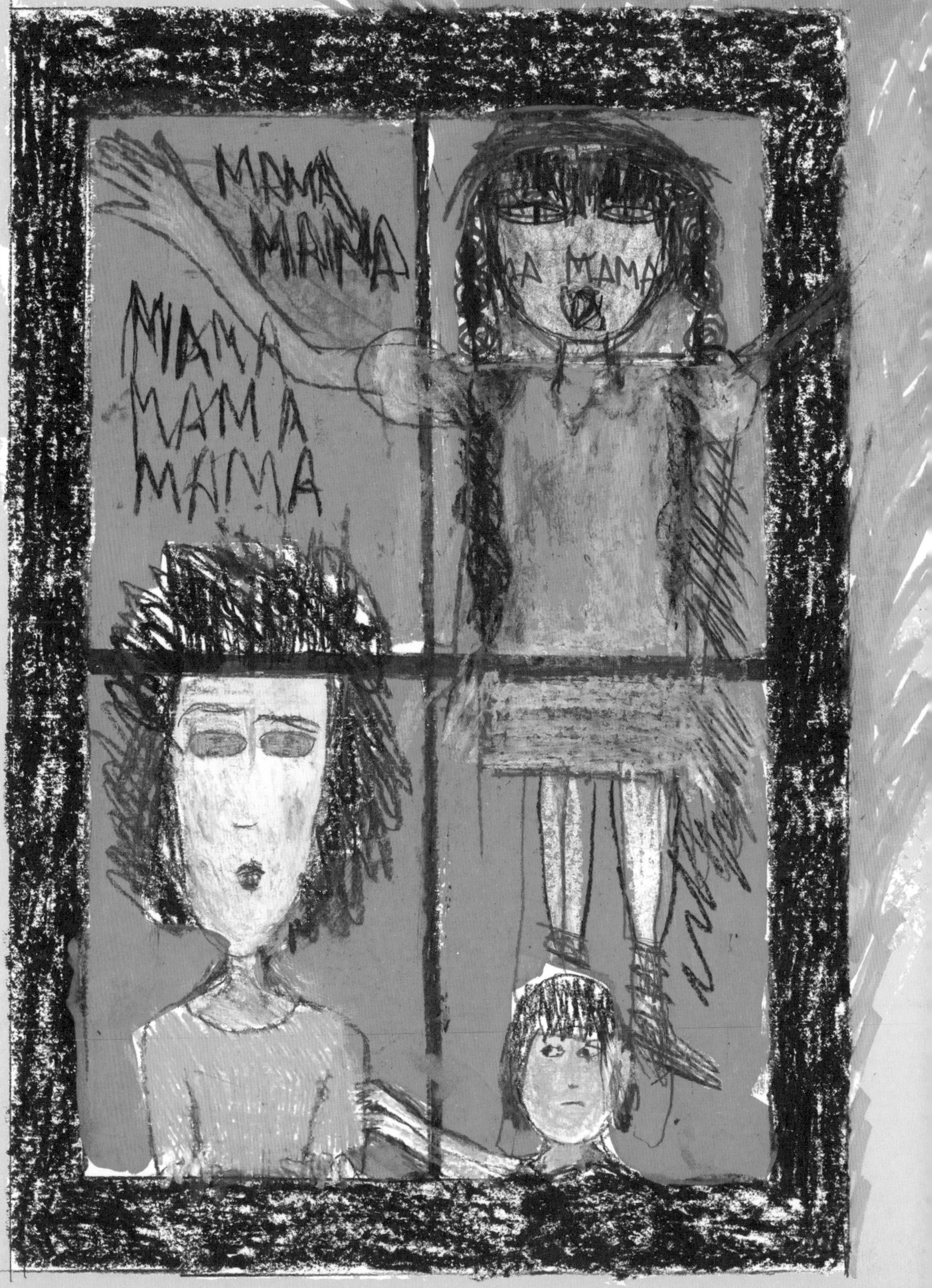
MAMA
MAMA
MAMA
MAMA
MAMA
MAMA

The three of us—Marlene, Marie Jo, and I—had a clubhouse. It was in a closet on Marlene's back porch. It was a tiny closet for tools. We managed to get a table inside and of course a candle.

On a Saturday, Marlene went into the clubhouse alone and lit the candle, and in the narrow confines of the closet, her dress went up in flames. My mother and I saw her from our dining room window. We were two houses away; we could see her but not reach her.

My mother screamed, but she was barefoot, whirling around looking for her shoes. Marlene's mother heard her daughter from the kitchen and she beat out the flames with her bare hands.

What happened to Marlene? Was she scarred? I remember nothing of the aftermath of the fire. I think if she had been badly burned we would have talked about nothing else. I dreamt about Marlene this year.

A friend is driving me to the Ragdale artists' colony in Lake Forest, Illinois,

AFteR the Fire

MY DREAM

Last night I dreamt of Marlene. In the dream I walked past Marlene's house. I could see inside as if it were a huge stage set, and there she was — an adult woman with short curly blonde hair. Nothing like the dark-haired beautiful child I knew. I called to her, and after a slight hesitation, she recognized me and invited me in to show me her daughter's work. Her daughter was an artist. Her paintings were not separate canvases; they were the walls. The interior was pale and transparent with streaks of color. Her images were the house.

where I will start work on this memoir of my childhood spent on the west side of Chicago.

I tell him the story of Marlene and the fire and how her mother heroically put out the flames on Marlene's clothing with her bare hands. He wonders if his mother would have done that for him. I say, "I wonder, too." But in fact I don't. I think of stories I heard of mothers who lift cars off their trapped children. Amazing feats of strength and sacrifice. I know my mother would be that mother.

Leaving the Neighborhood

BUT NOT IN STYLE

After the war, jobs became more plentiful, people started to make more money, and those little one-bedroom apartments began to seem cramped.

I knew about the existence of the suburbs, places that had ranch houses and big lawns, because my father drove outside the city on weekends. Those suburbs had nothing to do with me except for the time it took to drive there and back. I was drawing. Drawings that had nothing to do with what I drew later. Drawings of a preteen girl: elegant women with long graceful necks, and later, pictures of Harry Belafonte from magazines.

I graduated from Senn High School and went off to University of Illinois in Urbana/Champaign, where the tuition was practically nothing, and I borrowed money without interest and paid it back over a long period of time. I was seventeen and my uncles would often make this witty remark: "So you're off to college to get your MRS degree?" I was livid. In my experience aunts don't make that kind of joke.

So I went to the University of Illinois. In my last year I met a teaching assistant in my sociology class who lived in Chicago and was going there for the summer and so was I, and I dated him, and then we married.

I refused to have a religious ceremony, so I was married by a judge. A poem by Kahlil Gibran was very popular then, and there was a line in that poem that appealed to me: "You will be as one, but there will be spaces in your oneness." (Probably this is not quite the line, but the sentiment is right.)

The judge refused to read that poem; he felt it was anti-marriage. My mother had rented the hall at the country club, my cousin was playing the piano, the invitations were out, and the sign on the bulletin board read "Shirley Garrison's Party," so I got married.

Paul got an assistant professorship at Harvard. This was not a job that led to becoming a full professor, it was an enticement to young scholars to spend a few years teaching at Harvard and then become a professor at a lesser college.

Meanwhile, I applied and was accepted at Boston University for an MFA in painting. This time my degree was followed by a divorce—an exotic divorce, because I had to go to Mexico for it, because I went by myself and stayed in a hotel in El Paso, and because I was driven across the border and into a grand government building without a word being said by the driver and then silently motioned up many stairs, where I was sure I would be murdered because no one in the world knew where I was. I held my breath until I was led into a room with many flags and an older man sitting behind a desk, who divorced me

along with two other supplicants from New York.

We all signed our flowery certificates and had enchiladas for lunch.

Marriage took me to Massachusetts and divorce sent me back to Chicago where the jobs were. I became a graphic designer and illustrator. The first job I got was to redesign a feminist magazine called *The Spokeswoman*. It was a national newsletter. The women who ran it wanted it to look more like a real magazine and I found the first place for my illustration and graphic design.

After *The Spokeswoman* published a calendar of my cartoons, an anti-war magazine in New York interviewed me. This interview brought me to the attention of a New York editor who was emboldened by the success of a recent book of hers about women's sexuality and wanted to publish a book of my cartoons. Her committee, made up of middle-aged men, thought that a woman cartoonist was an oxymoron and rejected the book.

Knowing very little about New York, I asked this editor to find me another publisher or an agent over the weekend. She introduced me to a senior editor at St. Martin's Press. He went to bat for me and they published my cartoon collection.

Much to my surprise I became a syndicated cartoonist, publishing a cartoon strip with a sardonic middle-aged character called Sylvia with great pleasure for thirty-five years.

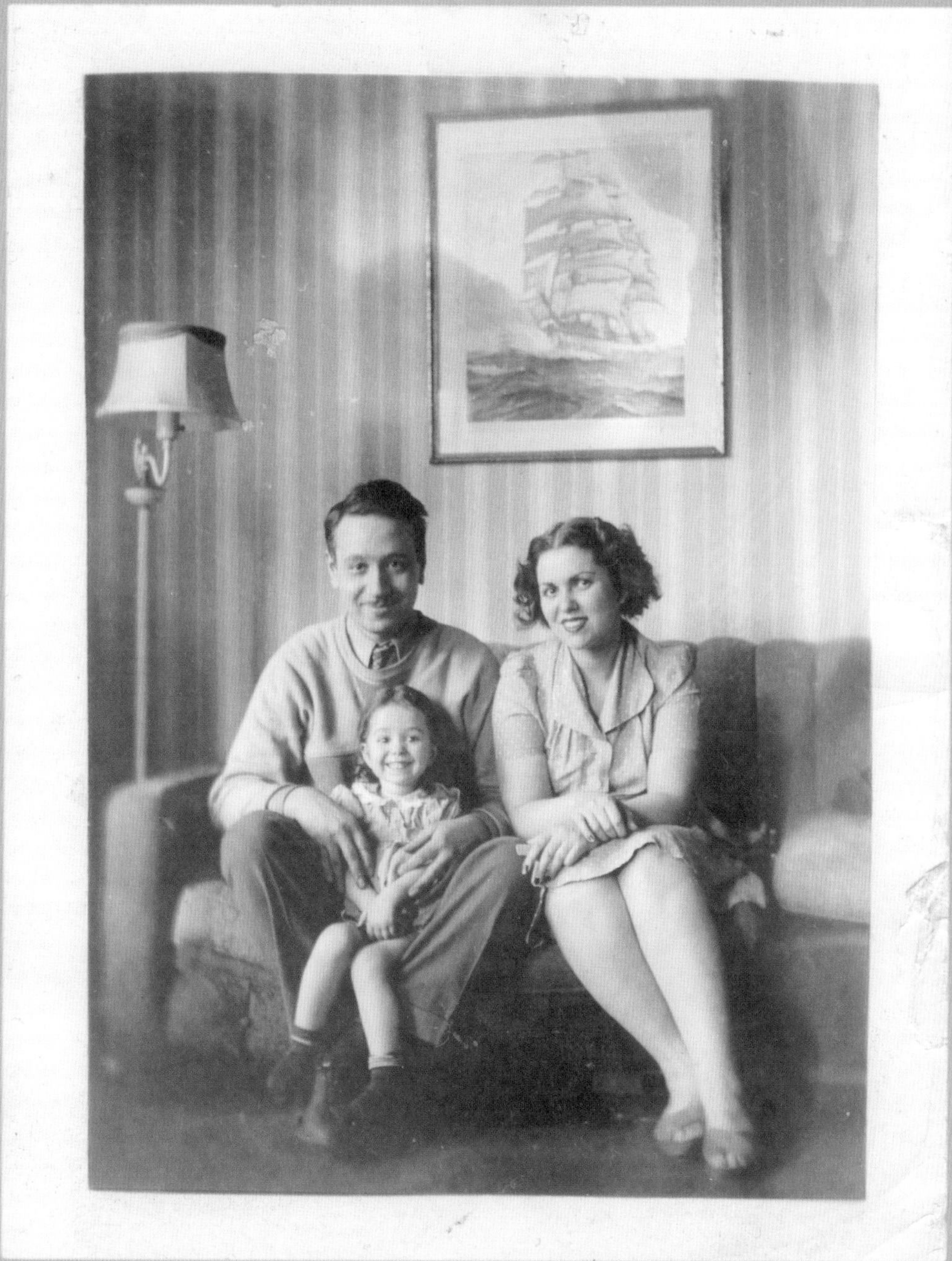

Epilogue

WHERE DID THE CATS COME FROM?

A cat as a pet? I remained ignorant of the possibility until I was forty years old. My discovery of cats was simultaneous with my becoming a cartoonist. Can this be an accident? Or is there some greater design at work?

My next-door neighbor had two cats. It was my birthday. She suggested that we follow up on a classified ad offering kittens to a loving, suitable home. Well, I was certainly suitable enough. We drove to an elegant-looking apartment hotel on LaSalle Street and rang the bell. We opened the door and were knocked flat by the odor of cat urine. We were in a room with an ornately carved loveseat covered in ripped and stained upholstery. The only other object in the room was a professional photograph of a beautiful young woman.

The woman, no longer young, opened the door from an adjacent room and carried in two kittens. One, a tortoise cat, looked like a mad woman—that was Harriet—and then a very calm—too calm—cat, John, who looked like he belonged in a barbershop quartet. His calmness was due to an infection, and Harriet had ear mites, perhaps why she looked wild-eyed. I signed a form saying I would never keep them out of any room they wanted to be in, and they were mine. And soon after, I signed a contract with the Sun-Times Media Syndicate and produced my first *Sylvia* cartoon strip in 1980.